OLWEUS®
BULLYING PREVENTION PROGRAM

Class Meetings That Matter

A Year's Worth of Resources for Grades 6–8

Vicki Crocker Flerx, Ph.D.
Susan P. Limber, Ph.D.
Nancy Mullin, M.Ed.
Jane Riese, L.S.W.
Marlene Snyder, Ph.D.
Dan Olweus, Ph.D.

HAZELDEN®

naespfoundation
ENDOWING LEADERSHIP AND LEARNING

Hazelden
Center City, Minnesota 55012
hazelden.org

ISBN: 978-1-59285-831-6

13 12 11 10   2 3 4 5 6

Cover design by David Spohn
Interior design and typesetting by Ryan Scheife, Mayfly Design

What Is the Purpose of This Manual?

The purpose of this manual is to provide teachers and other school staff members with developmentally appropriate activities to use as part of their *OBPP* class meetings in grades 6–8. These class meetings are grouped according to one of eight subject areas. When planning class meetings with your students, we encourage you to keep in mind several principles:

1. Even within these fairly narrow grade groupings, not all class meetings will be appropriate for each grade level or even each class within a grade. Choose class meetings as appropriate—make sure "prerequisite" class meetings are completed first so concepts build upon each other.

2. Although it is appropriate to revisit concepts regularly, class meetings should be varied in terms of how ideas are presented, and the focus of discussion. We hope that you will adapt and expand on ideas in this manual as appropriate for your students.

3. It is not expected that you complete all the class meetings each year at each grade level. Rather, we recommend that as a school you determine what sessions might be most appropriate at each grade level. There are a broad range of curriculum connections associated with each class meeting. It is not our expectation that you will cover all of these curriculum connections within any one class meeting.

4. Some class meetings may require more than one class period to complete. In such cases, be sure to leave some time at the end of each session to process the portion of the activity to that point and let students know what to expect during the next session.

5. Be creative! Utilize your own ideas and student feedback to put your own "stamp" on these class meetings. We also recommend that you link these class meetings and the underlying concepts to your academic content whenever possible.

This manual is not meant to be used as a stand-alone program. It should be used as part of a comprehensive, schoolwide implementation of the *Olweus Bullying Prevention Program*. The class meetings in this book build upon those provided in the *OBPP* Teacher Guide.

"*Class Meetings That Matter* is a long-awaited bullying prevention resource for sixth, seventh, and eighth graders. Use any of the guided activities/discussions for a real focus on peer pressure, social dilemmas, privilege, belonging, fairness, and safety for everyone, including ways to practice life skills that engage students and address campus issues."

—Kathy Middleton Morgan
Co-author of "Students' Perception of Bullying in Oklahoma
Public Schools," *Journal of School Violence* 8 (2009): 216–232.

"This resource book, designed for use in tandem with the *OBPP* Teacher Guide, offers schools a wide variety of class meeting topics on character traits and social skills—the development of which will empower students to reduce bullying. Topics are creatively addressed and sessions are designed as blueprints that teachers can tailor to the particular needs of their classes."

—Catherine F. (Katie) Moffett, Ed.D.
Director, Bully-Free Virginia

"This manual is an excellent tool that will serve to link the *Olweus Bullying Prevention Program* objectives to classroom teachers and their students. The activities are based in experiential practices, making them engaging and more meaningful for both students and their teachers."

—Mara Madrigal-Weiss, MA, MS
Student Support Services, San Diego County Office of Education,
Olweus Trainer (6 years)

Contents

Acknowledgments

Educators implementing the *Olweus Bullying Prevention Program* in the United States have been asking for more ideas for engaging students in conversations about bullying behaviors and other related topics during class meetings. (Initial class meeting topics and videos with discussion questions are included in the *OBPP* Teacher Guide.) We thank them for their dedication to bullying-prevention efforts and for providing time for students to discuss and consider topics important to improve school climate.

Our *Olweus Bullying Prevention Program* trainers provide training for schools' Bullying Prevention Coordinating Committees (BPCC) and provide basic information for setting ground rules and practice in conducting class meetings in their training agendas. We are proud of our trainers and thank them for their work with BPCC members to implement the program with fidelity, including training to support class meetings.

We would like to thank educators from all over the United States, including Matt Hague, James Miller, Sarah Radkowsky, and Alicia McDyre who provided invaluable feedback and suggestions for this collection of class meeting ideas.

In addition, Rebecca Ninke, Debbie Trafton O'Neal, and the editorial team of Pamela Foster and Sue Thomas at Hazelden Publishing helped shepherd the development of this curriculum. Without their support, creativity, and assistance, this project would not have been produced.

As a group of authors, we thank all our family members who continue to inspire and support our work.

Introduction

What Is the Olweus Bullying Prevention Program?

The *Olweus Bullying Prevention Program (OBPP)* is the most researched and best-known bullying prevention program available today. With over thirty-five years of research and successful implementation all over the world, *OBPP* is a whole-school program that has been proven to prevent or reduce bullying in schools.

OBPP is used at the school, classroom, and individual levels and includes methods to reach out to parents and the community for involvement and support. School administrators, teachers, and other staff are primarily responsible for introducing and implementing the program. These efforts are designed to improve peer relations and make the school a safer and more positive place for students to learn and develop.

What Is the Purpose of This Manual?

As part of *OBPP,* classroom teachers are asked to hold regular class meetings with students. The *OBPP* Teacher Guide provides outlines and suggested discussion questions for class meetings that are held as an initial part of this program.

This manual provides thirty-five additional class meetings for grades 6–8. The manual gives specific content for class meetings beyond the initial phases of implementation and into subsequent school years. The purpose of class meetings is to broaden bullying topics to include a variety of content related to peer relations.

The thirty-five class meetings are organized into eight categories. Within each category, class meetings are arranged in a specific order so as to build on one another. These categories include

- Building a Positive Classroom Climate (four class meetings)
- Identifying Feelings (four class meetings)
- Communication (six class meetings)
- Hot Spots (five class meetings)
- Peer Relationships (ten class meetings)
- Respecting Differences and Promoting Acceptance (three class meetings)

- Serving the Community/Reaching Outward (two class meetings)
- Using Current Events (one class meeting)

Because this manual is meant to be used as part of a comprehensive, schoolwide implementation of the *Olweus Bullying Prevention Program*, classroom teachers will want to review and apply the class meeting guidelines outlined in the *OBPP* Teacher Guide (chapter 6) before implementing ideas in this manual. It is recommended that every classroom teacher has a copy of this manual or, at a minimum, there should be one copy for every three teachers. If teachers must share, the Bullying Prevention Coordinating Committee can assist with a plan that facilitates teachers sharing this resource.

The class meeting activities in this manual are organized by topic. Although it is not necessary to follow topics in order, they are listed in a logical sequence so that concepts build on each other. Make sure students have covered "prerequisite" concepts first.

We recommend that class meetings not be repeated verbatim; that is, class meetings for grades 7 and 8 should not repeat exactly what was presented in grade 6. Students and teachers need variety in materials, activities, and follow-up discussion to keep class meetings fresh and interesting. We encourage teachers to be creative, and particularly to rely on student ideas, needs, and concerns, and to include student writing and age-appropriate literature as springboards for discussion.

A list of recommended resources is provided on pages 177–178 of this manual. We encourage you to use these resources as supplements to class meeting activities to provide variety.

How Are the Class Meetings Structured?

General guidelines for conducting class meetings appear in the *OBPP* Teacher Guide. In this manual, each class meeting is organized in the following structure:

Background Information

This brief paragraph provides insight into the purpose of the class meeting activity and issues teachers should be aware of as they facilitate the meeting. Information regarding prerequisite activities/concepts will also appear in this section.

Learner Outcomes

This text identifies the learning that will occur as a result of implementing the class meeting.

Materials Needed

This list contains the resources needed to conduct the class meeting. These materials have been kept to a minimum to make implementation easier. Any handouts on the materials list will be found in the manual following the class meeting outline.

Preparation Needed

This list will give you step-by-step instructions to prepare for the opening activity and follow-up discussion for the class meeting.

Class Meeting Outline

Each class meeting outline contains the following components: opening activity, discussion questions, and wrap-up. All text in the outline that is **bold** is scripted text. Facilitators may choose to read this text from the manual, use it as a guide, or not use it at all.

Opening Activity

This activity introduces the class meeting theme and gets students motivated and thinking about the topic. Opening activities last about half of the total class meeting time (a time frame is suggested for each). In some cases, the class meeting may require more than one class period and may be carried over from one week to another.

Discussion Questions

Following the opening activity are discussion questions to help students process the activity and apply it to their lives at school and outside of school. Questions are arranged in a general sequential order (from most basic to more in depth) and allow teachers to provide more nuanced discussions with students at different ability and age levels. Teachers should realize that they might not get through all of the discussion questions for each class meeting, and they might want to make adjustments according to student interest. Student discussion and debriefing is a key part of the class meeting, so allow most of the remaining meeting time for this.

Wrap-Up

Each class meeting includes a short wrap-up that should be used to summarize the key concepts discussed and provide an opportunity to extend the activity or student thinking about the topic.

Additional Components

Teacher Tips

These include strategies and resources to help the class meeting run smoothly. They are located in the margins.

Dig Deeper

These include concepts or ideas to further facilitator and/or student understanding. They are located in the margins.

Curriculum Connections

This section, found at the end of each class meeting outline, provides ideas for integrating the class meeting topic into other subject areas.

What Are Class Meetings?

Class meetings are an important component of *OBPP*. The purpose of these meetings is to build class cohesion and community, to teach the four anti-bullying rules, to help students understand the consequences of bullying and their role in bullying situations, and to address issues about bullying as they arise. At first, class meetings should focus on various aspects of bullying, but classroom teachers will also want to use these meetings to address additional related themes and topics.

There is no one right way to lead a class meeting. Some teachers prefer to have a step-by-step plan for what is going to be discussed. The class meeting activities in this manual serve that need. Other teachers are comfortable with a more open-ended style that provides flexibility to discuss issues as they come up. In this case, you will want to just use the class meeting activities as an outline. Either approach is fine.

This manual suggests a variety of methods to keep class meetings fresh and interesting for students and adults alike. Most teachers find these meetings relatively easy to conduct and a rewarding way to get to know their students better.

If you do not feel comfortable leading these meetings, members of your school's Bullying Prevention Coordinating Committee or your school's certified Olweus trainer could lead or co-lead the first couple of sessions. Or a teacher with experience in class meetings could co-lead as well.

More detailed information about conducting class meetings can be found in chapter 6 of the *OBPP* Teacher Guide. Again, it is important to hold the class meetings outlined in the Teacher Guide first, before using the class meeting activities in this manual.

Setting basic ground rules for these class meetings is important so that students feel safe in sharing their concerns and all members of the class feel respected and heard. Suggested class meeting ground rules can be found on page 70 of the Teacher Guide.

What Is the Difference between Curriculum Lessons and Class Meetings?

Class meetings are not the same as curriculum lessons. Although you have information you want to share with students, a class meeting is designed to establish communication among all members of your class. You will want to provide time for students to share their opinions and allow students to guide the discussion when appropriate. Class meetings are not a new concept. Many people in the education field have researched and documented this method for years.

Your role in leading class meetings is more of facilitator than teacher. This does not mean you will not guide the discussion. You will need to make sure your discussion goals are met through the careful use of probing and open-ended questioning. Class meetings are an opportunity for students to share their feelings and opinions and to suggest solutions as they learn about how to follow the rules, interact as a community, and handle bullying situations appropriately.

Remember, as a facilitator, you should

- be an attentive listener (student contributions are the main focus of class meetings)
- make sure the viewpoints of all students are heard
- make sure everyone has the opportunity to speak and that certain individuals do not dominate the conversation
- remind students who interrupt about the ground rules set up at the beginning of your class meetings

What Steps Should Be Taken to Organize and Lead Class Meetings?

When planning and leading your class meetings, keep the following in mind:

- It works best to have students sit in a circle or half circle so that they can see as well as hear each other. Students could be on the floor or in chairs or desks.
- Class meetings should be held regularly, preferably at least once a week. For middle school students, the meetings could last 30 to 40 minutes.
- It works best to have meetings at a specific time each week. Your school's Bullying Prevention Coordinating Committee may want all class meetings to be held on the same day. Check with the committee before starting your meetings.
- Within any given class meeting, you may want to switch from large-group to small-group activities. This keeps the meetings interesting. Many of the meetings in this manual suggest both large-group and small-group activities.
- Don't allow students to intimidate others during the meetings. Take the lead in reinforcing the message that all bullying incidents will be taken seriously and addressed either by you or the other staff at your school. Also stress that if you hear about any retaliation for what is said by students during a class, there will be consequences.
- If you want to bring up a specific bullying problem in your classroom, be sure all students involved have given permission to do so. In these cases, names may be used, but manage this situation and the resulting discussion so all students are respected and the focus is on positive solutions.
- Be aware that you will likely have students who are being bullied by others in your group. Do not force students to talk about their experiences unless they feel comfortable doing so and unless you are prepared to facilitate this discussion. Be sensitive to the painfulness of bullying and the tremendous impact it can have on students. Do not make light of bullying situations and do not allow other students to do so either.
- Evaluating your class meetings will help to refine them and improve their effectiveness. Use the Class Meeting Activity Log on the *OBPP* Teacher Guide CD-ROM (document 19) for these evaluation purposes.

- In every class meeting, suspend the discussion outline for relevant digressions and questions. Students may have bullying issues that they want to work out in a safe environment.

Why Is Role-Playing an Important Part of Class Meetings?

Several of the activities in this manual involve role-playing. An *OBPP* research study has shown that teachers who systematically used role-playing in their anti-bullying work obtained larger reductions in bullying problems than those who did not. Role-playing

- gives students insights into the different types of bullying and what roles bystanders, followers, and defenders might take in each situation
- helps students develop a better emotional understanding of how the different participants feel in bullying situations and what motivates them to do what they do
- provides a springboard for discussions about bullying and ways to stop it
- provides valuable opportunities for students to practice, test, and evaluate solutions to bullying situations. When students act out positive behaviors, they also model them for others. It can be especially powerful for students to see social leaders in the classroom reject bullying or intervene in a bullying situation.

Chapter 7 in the Teacher Guide provides detailed information about how to conduct role-plays so that students are respected and positive messages are conveyed. Be sure to read through this chapter before doing any role-plays.

What Should You Do If, during a Class Meeting, a Student Reveals That He or She Has Been Bullied?

Whenever you are talking about real bullying incidents during your class meetings, it is helpful to suggest that students not use names or too many details. This is done to protect students.

Occasionally during a class meeting a student may reveal that he or she is being bullied. It is best to ask the student to talk with you privately after the class meeting about this situation. Be sure to follow up with the student to find out what has been happening. You may need to report this incident to your school's administration. Check with your school's Bullying Prevention Coordinating Committee to determine the appropriate reporting procedures.

How Are Class Meetings Linked to Academic Curricula?

Although class meetings are not the same as curriculum, learning is still occurring during these meetings. Learner outcomes are provided with each meeting for this reason. Teachers are also encouraged to extend the learning during class meetings by linking the topics to academic subjects such as health, English, history, social studies, science, and communications.

What Else Should You Keep in Mind When Conducting Class Meetings?

- Use both large- and small-group discussions. If your students are less communicative during large-group discussions, you can always have them break into smaller groups. Typically, as students get to know one another better, their comfort level in large-group discussions increases.
- Allow students to spend the time needed to explore these concepts. Many sessions may have content that extends beyond a single class meeting. If you would like to expand any of the sessions into future class meetings, you are encouraged to do so.
- Many class meetings encourage students to try out strategies and implement ideas that come out of the discussions. Be sure to follow up with these suggestions during future class meetings.

Using These Class Meetings Across Grade Levels

Because the class meetings in this manual are designed for students in multiple grade levels, it is important to consider the developmental needs of your students and adjust how each class meeting activity is presented and how the resulting discussion is led. There are more ideas and alternative discussion questions than can be covered in a single session. This is purposeful in order to allow teachers to revisit concepts and class meetings over different grade levels, without repeating material. In addition, linking class meetings to grade-appropriate student literature or other academic content will allow opportunities for greater variation.

Students in grades 6–8 have some developmental characteristics in common that are relevant to conducting these class meetings. These are summarized here.

Grades 6–8

- Because peer acceptance is so important, adults need to be aware of biases that can occur so that they can support vulnerable students. Positive peer pressure can also be employed as a strategy for preventing and responding to bullying.
- Students of this age may resist boundaries set by adults, but they also find comfort and reassurance in them.
- Rapidly changing bodies can result in feelings of self-consciousness, and they also may be a source of bullying.
- Their expanding worldview makes this an ideal time to look at issues of social justice related to bullying, as well as power imbalances in relationships.
- Students are pleased about affirmation from adults as long as it doesn't embarrass them; this is important to keep in mind when deciding on ways to reinforce positive social behavior, such as stepping in to help someone being bullied.
- The fact that they are influenced by and spend more time with friends provides opportunities to talk about the effects of peer pressure on social choices and using courage to make better choices.

Respecting Differences and
Promoting Acceptance for Others

As you prepare and lead the three class meetings on respecting differences and promoting acceptance for others (see pages 148–160), read through these definitions and ideas.

The Importance of Teaching Tolerance and Acceptance for Others

We live in a diverse society and in a world where teaching children to live peacefully with others is becoming increasingly more important. The *OBPP* philosophy is one of ensuring basic human rights. Promoting empathy for others and promoting tolerance for diversity are closely tied to this value. Teaching about tolerance and acceptance of differences is perhaps one of the most important pathways to peace, not only in our world, but in our schools and communities. Participating in age-appropriate discussions about respecting differences and accepting diversity is an important element of a child's basic education that can reduce stereotypes and prejudice. School administrators, whether in socially or economically diverse districts or not, should ensure that all teachers have opportunities to participate in training about how to approach teaching these important concepts. The more teachers feel knowledgeable about these ideas, the more comfortable they will be approaching this subject and addressing issues of discrimination, stereotyping, and bigotry.

Additional Things to Keep in Mind

- The issue of how to address respect for differences and promote tolerance and acceptance goes well beyond the scope of this manual, but is relevant as a broad bullying-prevention issue in two important ways. First, intolerance of any kind impinges on individual human rights. Second, it contributes to and can create a negative school climate where students are unable to fully focus on learning.

- While some schools may have student bodies that represent diversity in several or many areas (cultural, ethnic, linguistic, religious, socio-economic, or family constellations), many schools have very little diversity.

- Teaching about tolerance is not a topic important only to those in "diverse" school communities. Children and adults should be encouraged to view their school community as part of a more global community as a way of preparing them to live in a peaceful society.

- The class meetings in this manual are not intended as a substitute for teaching children about diversity or respect and acceptance for others, but are instead meant to raise awareness about the roles that stereotypes, privilege, and prejudice play in bullying and bullying prevention.

- Discuss any acts of intolerance directly, concretely, and in ways that are related to students' real-life experiences.

- School provides students with an important window to the wider world—beyond what they can see and experience every day. However, true diversity education is more than acknowledging differences and sampling aspects through a "cultural awareness fair" approach. It is more meaningful and effective to strengthen communication and a sense of connection within the school so that students and adults have a strong base from which they can talk about issues that can potentially divide them, lead to exclusion and bullying, or escalate into stereotypes that marginalize, prejudice, discrimination, and hate.

- Discussions about valuing diversity and differences can become misguided when they focus too heavily on individual uniqueness, too-subtle differences (a special learning need that may not be outwardly visible, for example), or experiences that are too far removed from students' daily life to be genuinely meaningful to them (such as general discussions about cultures around the world or isolated "cultural awareness fairs").

- Be aware of how diversity is demonstrated in textbooks and reading lists in your curriculum. Highlight instances where sensitivity to diversity is lacking and offer supplemental materials where appropriate. In reading classes, use works from a variety of cultures and perspectives.

- Many studies have shown that children as young as age three have picked up terms of prejudice without really understanding their significance.

- As part of normal development, children notice differences and form attachments to others they perceive as like them. Early in life, many children acquire a full set of biases that can be observed in verbal slurs and acts of discrimination.

How to Define the Terms Used in These Class Meetings

It is important to explain terminology to students in age-appropriate terms. The following terms are used in the class meetings on respecting differences and promoting acceptance of others. Definitions are provided here to help teachers relate these concepts to bullying-prevention themes.

- **Stereotype:** An exaggerated belief, image, or distorted truth about a person or group. Stereotypes encourage people to think about others based on inflexible and incorrect ideas. These generalizations do not allow for individual differences. Stereotypes are often portrayed or reinforced through images in mass media, or beliefs passed on by family or community members. Stereotypes about gender (and what is considered "normal" behavior or appearance for boys and girls) are particularly prevalent in our society and play a critical role in acceptance and treatment of bullying behavior.

- **Prejudice:** An opinion, prejudgment, or attitude about a group or its individual members. Prejudices are often associated with ignorance, fear, or hatred. Social scientists believe children begin to acquire prejudices and stereotypes as toddlers.

- **Discrimination:** Behavior that treats people unfairly and unequally because of the group to which they belong. Discriminatory behaviors range from subtle and seemingly harmless slights and exclusion to more obvious hate crimes. Discrimination often begins with negative stereotypes and prejudices.

- **Respect:** Can be defined with synonyms such as "to value," "to appreciate," "to care about," "to be considerate of," or "to show consideration for." Many students are more familiar with the word *respect* when used in a very different context, such as "respect your elders," which implies following, obeying, or deferring to another. Reinforcing the notions of respect as valuing each other is more in keeping with both diversity training and bullying-prevention concepts.

Optional Activities and Resources

1. You may wish to take part in Mix It Up at Lunch Day, a nationwide campaign that supports students who want to identify, question, and cross social boundaries that separate them from each other and help build inclusive, welcoming learning environments. On Mix It Up at Lunch Day, schools and students use creative ways to "mix it up" in the cafeteria, helping kids break out of their usual seating patterns and get to know new people. Information about organizing this activity can be found at www .tolerance.org/teens/.

2. The following Web sites and books can provide resources for your class meetings, including in-depth explorations of the importance of tolerance, and dealing with bigotry and prejudice.

- Anti-Defamation League: www.adl.org/default.htm
- Children's Defense Fund: www.childrensdefense.org
- Southern Poverty Law Center: www.tolerance.org
- Global Classroom Connection: www.classroom-connection.org
- The North Carolina Center for Diversity Education: www.diversityed.org
- Books: *Asperger Syndrome and Bullying: Strategies and Solutions* (Nick Dubin), *Perfect Targets: Asperger Syndrome and Bullying; Practical Solutions for Surviving the Social World* (Rebekah Heinrichs and Brenda Smith Myles)

Ideas and Strategies for Grouping Students

Generally, class meetings are conducted with the entire class sitting in a circle. For some sessions, you will be encouraged to have students work in smaller groupings for at least part of the session and then return back together in a circle to process the activity as a class.

Used effectively, small groups can enhance opportunities for communication and cooperation, support development of interpersonal skills and relationship-building, and foster trust and teamwork—all of which reinforce *OBPP* goals for bullying prevention. Unfortunately, group work can also cause tension and conflict for students when assigned groupings reinforce existing social hierarchies or exacerbate problem behaviors, such as bullying. Students at all levels need guidance from adults to learn to work with others who have different styles or viewpoints, to take leadership without being bossy, or to articulate feelings and ideas in socially acceptable ways. Teachers who are aware of potential issues within a particular group of students are better able to make adjustments so *OBPP* activities run smoothly. While carefully considering how to assign groups may initially take some planning on the part of adults, positive results will carry over into building positive class relationships.

Tips for Forming Groups

As much as possible, opt for variety and balance groups by gender, ethnic group, personalities, learning styles, and social diversity; but be mindful of balancing group dynamics, power imbalances, and shared biases.

1. Avoid groupings that reinforce biases or social hierarchies in your class (boys against girls, for example).
2. Provide structure, support, and guidance for students with learning or social difficulties, impulse control, making social connections, or a tendency to withdraw or be "slow-to-warm-up."
3. To ensure inclusion and opportunities for all students to experience working with all members of the class, students need to be assigned to particular partners or groupings.

4. Offer different options for pairings or groupings to provide students a variety of opportunities to interact with different class members and to minimize being "stuck" in a group with poor dynamics.

5. Practice using a variety of approaches for forming or identifying groups: symbols, colors, shapes, activity (such as reading buddy partner), or randomly assigned by counting off using numbers or words (such as "We, Will, Not, Bully, Others").

6. Once students are familiar with groupings, save time by instructing them to "Get into your anti-bullying rules pairings," or "Let's use our color groups for this meeting."

Tips for Maximizing Group Effectiveness

1. Promote teamwork by beginning group projects with icebreaker questions that help students learn more about each other.

2. Consider what each group member has to offer and what skills each needs to develop.

3. Traditional group roles (leader, captain, reporter, and so on) often go to popular or more verbal students, reinforcing existing social hierarchies among students. Teachers can assign roles that emphasize individual talents, and reinforce more even participation.

   - Non-hierarchical roles can be:
     - content-related (information gatherer, question asker, challenger)
     - product-related (artistic consultant, spell checker, fact checker, quality control manager, artistic advisor)
     - process-related (discussion starter, agenda maker, recorder, documenter, timekeeper, quality control manager, presenter, peacekeeper)
   - Discuss vocabulary and what each role entails in advance.

4. Provide support and concrete ground rules for working through common pitfalls of group work, such as uneven participation, negotiating differences of opinions, and so on.

Category 1

Building a Positive Classroom Climate

(Four class meetings)

Grades 6–8

Category: Building a Positive Classroom Climate

Topic: Team-Building among Students

Do I Know You?

Background

Students' relationships shift dramatically during the middle school years. In addition, normal adolescent development can heighten students' sense of alienation from their peers at a time when relationships become even more essential to them. Caring adults can help students navigate these transitions and help them break down anxieties and barriers that separate them from peers. Interviewing classmates provides a way to practice building relationships, understanding, and empathy. Learning about each other facilitates openness and inclusion and improves the likelihood that students will act positively as bystanders in bullying situations.

Because team-building helps to promote trust and communication, it is recommended that the first two class meetings (Do I Know You? and Create Your Own!) be held early in the school year.

Learner Outcomes

By the end of this session, students will be able to
- list new things they learned about their classmates
- describe how having more in-depth knowledge about classmates promotes perspective-taking and acceptance

Materials Needed

- Paper and pencils for each student
- Chalkboard and chalk or dry erase board and markers

Preparation Needed

- Because students will interview each other, carefully consider class dynamics and create a list of pairing assignments. (See pages 13–14 for ideas and strategies for grouping students.) When students are allowed to pick partners or groups themselves, they often select the students they know best. If you have an uneven number of students, you may need to invite another student for this activity or be an interview partner.

Teacher Tip

The goal of this activity is to get to know others better. Assign students interview partners that encourage them to get to know someone from outside their circle of friends. Be careful not to pair vulnerable students with those who might be tormenters.

- Choose four to five questions from the following list that students will ask each other. Write the questions you choose on the board.
  - In which state or country were you born?
  - Have you been in school in other states or countries? If so, where?
  - What do you enjoy most on your vacations from school?
  - Do you have any hobbies or collections? What are they?
  - What kind of animals or pets do you like best?
  - If you had a couple of hours of free time to participate in any of the following activities, which would you choose? Would you choose to participate in an athletic activity, play or listen to music, play video games, or watch a movie?
  - Do you do any volunteer activities in the community? Which ones?
  - What kinds of music do you enjoy? What is your favorite singer/musical group? Favorite song?
  - What kind of work (or occupation) do you want to do when you are out of school?

Class Meeting Outline

Opening Activity (15 minutes)

1. **Today we are going to find out more about each other by conducting interviews. You will be paired up with another person and will ask the questions I have written on the board. When you are being interviewed, you should answer the questions and add any other information that you wish to share. You will have five minutes to interview your partner and then he or she will have five minutes to ask you the same questions.**

2. Announce interview pairings.

3. Allow students 10 minutes to interview their partner (5 minutes for each interview) and then come back in a circle to discuss and debrief.

Discussion Questions (15 minutes)

1. **What interesting things did you learn about your interview partner?**
2. **Were there things that surprised you or that you didn't expect?**
3. **Were there any funny stories in your interviews that can be shared with the group?**
4. **What are advantages of getting to know more about each other? What are disadvantages about assuming things about someone before we get to know that person?**
5. **How might questions like these help you to make friends with someone who is in a different circle of friends than you?**

Wrap-Up

1. **Sometimes we think we have someone figured out, but we are surprised to learn he or she is different than we thought. Others in class may have things in common with us that we didn't know about, or they may have talents or interests that surprise us. As a class, we need to make an effort to get to know each other as individuals.**

   One of the ways to stop bullying in our school is to help students understand that kids they don't know may not be so different from themselves. We all have a stake in the positive social life of this school. When bullying happens, it hurts every single one of us by limiting our opportunities for friendships and support.

2. Encourage additional questions and comments.

Curriculum Connections

Vocabulary: *assumptions, interview, open-ended questions, perspective-taking, preconceived notions*

English:

- Ask students to observe or read about different ways that journalists gather and convey information about their subjects.

- Have students select one or two questions that were not discussed and write responses to share in small-group discussion in subsequent class meetings.

Math: In small groups, have students make a list of similarities and differences they have learned about each other (include likes and dislikes, members of family, etc.) and plot results on graphs.

English or Science: Talk about how different types of questions can be used to gather different types of information (such as open-ended versus forced-choice).

Social Studies: Encourage students to interview a student or adult who has recently moved into the community, a person who has recently immigrated to this country, or a person whose first language or ethnicity isn't the same as their own.

Grades 6–8

Category: Building a Positive Classroom Climate

Topic: Team-Building among Students

Create Your Own!

Background

It is a relief for a student to look around a crowded hallway, a full bus, the cafeteria, or a new class and see a familiar face—someone the student can approach and talk to instead of standing alone or feeling isolated. Unfortunately, at least one or more students in your classroom will feel disconnected from peers at some point or another. Some may even feel bullied by others. Forging connections among your students will help to build relationships and make it less likely that they are bullied.

Because team-building helps to promote trust and communication, it is recommended that the first two class meetings (Do I Know You? and Create Your Own!) be held early in the school year.

Learner Outcomes

By the end of this session, students will be able to

- demonstrate they can work cooperatively in a group
- describe the benefits and importance of listening to each other
- demonstrate positive ways of taking leadership and responsibility

Materials Needed

- Paper and pencils for each team

Preparation Needed

None

Class Meeting Outline

Opening Activity (25–30 minutes)

1. **Working in small groups and doing team-building activities can help develop a safe, trusting environment in which we all can learn. Today we are going to take that one step further. You will be working in teams to create your own team-building activity or game.**

2. Split the group into teams of four to five students. (See pages 13–14 for ideas and strategies for grouping students.) Distribute paper and pencils to each group.

Teacher Tip

Resist leading the teams, and allow the students to strategize and work together.

3. **Each team will design a game or activity that small groups can do together. Use your creativity! These new activities can be physical, mental, non-verbal, funny, or anything else, as long as they are appropriate and are something that will help build trust with any small group. Ideas include writing new lyrics to a well-known song, using vocabulary words to create a crossword puzzle, using paper or cardboard squares to create a structure, or writing new rules to an existing sport (such as football, softball, baseball, or bowling). Write an explanation and the rules for the game or activity on your paper.**

4. **You will have 15 minutes to design your game or activity.**

5. As the teams work to create their small-group activities, circulate and offer help, if needed.

6. When time is up, bring the group back together, and have each team explain their game and the rules, so that the other teams can try them.

Discussion Questions (15–20 minutes)

1. **What were the biggest challenges your team faced in designing your game or activity?**

2. **What things helped you to work together as a team? What things didn't help?**

3. **Would all of the activities help build trust with small groups?**

4. **Without saying which ones, were there any games or activities that you would do with your own group of friends?**

5. **How does working together to create something help build trust and confidence in each other?**

6. **How does trying a new game or activity that someone else created help build trust and confidence in each other?**

7. **How can this help you outside of this classroom, in your everyday lives?**

Wrap-Up

1. **It's fun to be challenged, but we all need each other's help and guidance sometimes. When we cooperate and work together as a team to help each other out, we are all stronger.**

2. Encourage additional comments and questions.

Curriculum Connections

Vocabulary: *navigate, obstacle, responsibility, strategize, teamwork, trust*

English:

- Have students write about a time when they played a new, challenging game for the first time. Were they nervous? Did they catch on quickly? With whom did they play the game?

- Encourage students to write up the explanations and rules they came up with for their games and activities.

Physical Education: Plan a day to take more time to do all of the activities and games designed by the students in this class meeting.

Grades 6–8

Category: Building a Positive
Classroom Climate

Topic: How Your Class Can
Influence Others in a
Positive Way

Stopping Bullying Starts Here

Background

The term "peer pressure" often has a negative connotation. This class meeting highlights positive aspects of peer pressure. By creating their own anti-bullying message, students will be exerting positive peer pressure in your school. Encourage their instinct for activism to help end bullying.

Learner Outcomes

By the end of this session, students will be able to
- describe the forms of bullying reported in your school Olweus Bullying Questionnaire (OBQ) results (data available from school's Bullying Prevention Coordinating Committee)
- describe why students bully and the role peer pressure plays
- promote anti-bullying messages in your school community by creating a public service announcement (PSA)

Materials Needed

- Paper and pencils
- Chalkboard and chalk or dry erase board and markers
- Your school's OBQ results

Preparation Needed

- Make sure each student has paper and a pencil.
- Read through and select data from the school's OBQ, especially regarding the incidence of different kinds of bullying, the likelihood that bullied students tell an adult, and how students feel when they see another student being bullied. (See OBQ questions 5–12, 19, and 37.)
- Highlight some key findings from the school's OBQ on the board for the activity.

Class Meeting Outline

Opening Activity (25+ minutes)

1. **Today, we're going to look at some of our school data from the Olweus Bullying Questionnaire.**
2. **What are ways peer pressure plays a role in causing bullying?**
3. If possible, show a public service announcement about bullying from the Health Resources and Services Administration (www.stopbullying now.hrsa.gov) or the National Crime Prevention Council (www.ncpc .org/newsroom/current-campaigns/bully-prevention/). Discuss briefly what PSAs are and emphasize that PSAs are short. Most PSAs are only 15 to 30 seconds long.
4. Break the class into small groups of two to four students. (See pages 13–14 for ideas and strategies for grouping students.) Point out the OBQ results you highlighted on the board. Remind small-group members that they will be creating their own anti-bullying public service announcement using data from the OBQ.
5. Give each group time to write out the PSAs that will be presented.
6. Invite the groups to take turns "airing" their PSAs in front of the classroom. Offer helpful hints or edits as needed. After all the groups have presented, discuss the message of their PSAs.

Teacher Tip

Avoid "bully" and "victim" language. Instead, incorporate phrases like "a student who bullies" or "a student who is bullied" into your class dialogue and student commercials.

Discussion Questions (10 minutes)

1. **In what ways can bullying affect the morale of a classroom? a school?**
2. **What role do students play in encouraging bullying?**
3. **How can we use peer pressure for good?**
4. **How can our class contribute to improving morale so our school feels safer and accepting to all students?**
5. **Results from a study point out that just 5 percent of people in a crowd can influence the crowd's direction—and that the other 95 percent follow without realizing it.[1] How can we increase the percentage of students in this school who create a positive influence to stop bullying?**

Teacher Tip

Encourage students to consider gender, social class, and ethnic and/or racial groups when thinking of ways to make their school more accepting.

Wrap-Up

1. **You have the potential to be a positive or negative influence in our class, school, and community. I hope this class meeting has helped you see ways each of you can have a very positive effect.**
2. Encourage additional questions and comments.

Curriculum Connections

Vocabulary: *clique, morale, public service announcement, social class, sound bite*

English: Have students write a letter to a brother, sister, neighbor, or friend describing the school's bullying prevention program.

Social Studies: As part of a discussion about lobbying for change in a democracy, help students identify a way to use their anti-bullying PSAs to lobby for school change. One way might be to ask the principal to allow students to broadcast their PSAs during the morning or closing announcements each day.

Math/Science: Use the OBQ to teach students how to read and interpret simple frequency data. Have them use the data to create their own graphs. Based on their data, encourage students to develop their own hypotheses about bullying in their school. Students may also develop their own questions and interview other students to gather information and compare their results to school data.

Computer Science/Health: Have students use the Internet to research national bullying data and suggestions to address bullying. Use government and nonprofit educational Web sites such as:

- Olweus Bullying Prevention Program: www.olweus.org

- Stop Bullying Now!: www.stopbullyingnow.hrsa.gov

- National Crime Prevention Council: www.ncpc.org/newsroom/current-campaigns/bully-prevention/

Community Service/Drama/Arts:

- Suggest that students plan and execute an anti-bullying presentation to a younger grade in your school or district. They can use the OBPP four anti-bullying rules (found on page 51 of the Teacher Guide), the Bullying Circle from the Teacher Guide CD-ROM (document 18), or the definition of bullying (on page 11 of the Teacher Guide) as springboards for their presentation. Encourage them to incorporate creative ideas such as skits and raps into the presentation.

- Contact local community cable or radio stations to request that student PSAs be aired.

- Contact local stores to request that student slogans be featured on shopping bags or posters.

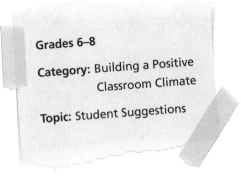

Grades 6–8

Category: Building a Positive
Classroom Climate

Topic: Student Suggestions

Bullying Behaviors in Me and You

Background

Bullying behavior is not always easy to identify; there often is a fine line between rough play and fighting and between verbal teasing and abusive language or gossip. This student-directed activity will help your class identify behaviors that "cross the line." This activity should follow class meetings on the four anti-bullying rules.

Learner Outcomes

By the end of this session, students will be able to
- distinguish between behaviors that are bullying and those that are not
- identify bullying behavior in themselves and others
- describe ways they can counter bullying behavior

Materials Needed

- Chalkboard and chalk or dry erase board and markers
- Paper and pencils
- Teacher Guide CD-ROM document 3 on the difference between bullying, rough-and-tumble play, and fighting

Preparation Needed

- Make a copy of document 3 for each group.

Class Meeting Outline

Opening Activity (15 minutes)

1. **There often can be a fine line between acceptable and unacceptable behaviors. Today's activity will help us tell the difference between bullying and non-bullying behaviors.**

2. Make four columns on the board. Head the columns Situation, Bullying, Not Bullying, Not Sure. Draw a horizontal line underneath the words.

3. Explain to the class that they will be moving into small groups. Each group will copy what you've written on the board and fill in the chart. In their groups, students will name a situation that they've been a part of or observed and write it down in that column on their chart, and then discuss whether they think it is "bullying" or "not bullying," or they're "not sure" and fill in the chart accordingly. Give examples such as the following:

   - You and your friend sometimes call each other names and laugh about it.
     - You overhear someone you know calling another student a nasty name.
     - You see someone shoving another classmate as they pass in the hall.
     - You see two friends pushing each other outside during gym class.
     - You receive an IM (instant message) from a classmate that says, "You're a loser! ☺"

4. Organize the class into small groups. Distribute the paper and a pencil to each group. Have someone in each group copy the chart on the board. Then have group members suggest situations and classify them in the columns on the paper.

5. Have a member of each group report on the group's chart and then discuss the following questions.

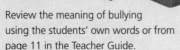

Teacher Tip

Review the meaning of bullying using the students' own words or from page 11 in the Teacher Guide.

Discussion Questions (15 minutes)

1. **How do you know when a behavior goes too far and becomes bullying?**
2. **Was there anything in your chart or discussion that surprised you?**
3. **Did all the members of your group agree? Did some of you feel some behaviors crossed the line? Did others feel differently?**
4. **What impact might this activity have on your behavior from now on?**
5. **Why do people have different tolerance levels for bullying behavior? (What did group members consider when deciding whether behavior crossed the line or not?) Was it easy to "know bullying when you see or hear it"? In the future, if you didn't know you were bullying someone and thought you were just "kidding around," what could you do to stop and change your actions?**
6. **What types of bullying have you seen around our school lately?**
7. **No one is perfect. We all say and do things that are wrong. When that happens, what can we do to correct our behavior and make amends to the person we hurt?**
8. **Have you ever become friends with someone you previously bullied or offended? Could you be friends with someone who had bullied or offended you? Why could or couldn't it feel like an equal friendship?**

Wrap-Up

1. **Bullying may be a common occurrence, but it is never acceptable, and it is against our school rules. Sometimes, we may have different ideas about when certain behaviors have crossed the line to become bullying.**

   If you see or hear bullying happening, step up to help or get help from an adult or other students. If you see or hear something and aren't sure if it is bullying or not, be on the safe side and tell an adult.

   If you go too far and bully other students, make an effort to take responsibility for your words and actions and stop your negative behaviors.
2. Encourage additional questions and comments.

Curriculum Connections

Vocabulary: *crossing the line, escalate, making amends, perception, responsibility for your own behavior, tolerance*

English:

- Use age-appropriate literature to highlight session concepts or to introduce the class meeting (such as *Tangerine* by Edward Bloor or *Stargirl* by Jerry Spinelli).

- Have students write about how they would feel if someone who had previously bullied them apologized. What would a genuine apology consist of or what else would they want from the person?

- Have students write about a time when they saw someone else being bullied or a time when they saw or heard negative behavior but weren't sure if it was bullying or not. How did this feel?

Health/Drama: Have students role-play examples of behaviors that cross the line to become bullying. Point out how body language can be a clue to distinguishing between bullying and non-bullying behavior.

Social Studies: Have students look through newspapers and magazines to find examples of bullying behavior in current events.

Category 2

Identifying Feelings

(Four class meetings)

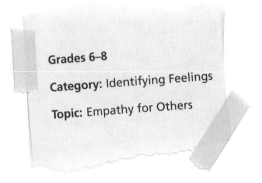

Grades 6–8

Category: Identifying Feelings

Topic: Empathy for Others

Empathy for Strangers and Friends

Background

Learning to show empathy helps us develop closer and deeper relationships with others. Middle school students need adult assistance to nurture and reinforce empathetic responses. At this age, students are aware of the impact their actions have on others, but they still need practice understanding the perspective of another person. Empathetic responses are important in spurring positive, defending action or involvement from bystanders, and in helping students who bully to curb their negative behaviors and make more positive choices.

Learner Outcomes

By the end of this session, students will be able to
- define empathy
- describe the role empathy plays in bullying situations
- identify ways they can show empathy toward others

Materials Needed

- Paper and pencils
- *Optional:* Dictionary
- Three large sheets of paper
- Chalkboard and chalk or dry erase board and markers

Preparation Needed

- Prepare three sheets of paper. On one, write Easy to Show Empathy, on the second write In Between, and on the third write Hard to Show Empathy. Post these along one long wall in your classroom or in three different corners. (Alternatively, write these categories on the board and ask students to silently vote for one of these three categories in #6 below.)

Class Meeting Outline

Opening Activity (15 minutes)

1. Write the word "empathy" on the board.
2. **How many of you know what "empathy" means?** Ask for a show of hands.
3. Explain the definition of empathy from a dictionary or use this one: **Empathy is identifying with the thoughts, feelings, or emotions of another person, especially in times of distress. It's like "walking in someone else's shoes."** Write a definition on the board.
4. Distribute pencils and paper. Challenge students to do the following individually:
   a. **Write a definition of "empathy" using your own words. What does it mean to you?**
   b. **Describe a time when someone showed empathy toward you.**
   c. **Describe a time when you missed an important opportunity to show empathy toward another.**
5. Invite students to share their definitions of empathy and to give examples of when empathy was shown or missed.
6. **Often, we find it easier to feel empathy toward some people than others.** Indicate the signs that you posted around the room. Read the following statements (or make up ones of your own). Ask students to stand by the signs you posted (or alternatively vote from their seats) to indicate how easy or difficult they believe it would be to show empathy for

Dig Deeper

- Empathy is more than simply understanding another's emotions. It involves vicariously experiencing the feelings, thoughts, and experiences of another. It results in compassion and a desire to help rather than hurt. It also involves understanding what kind of response would be most meaningful to the other person—and responding accordingly, even if it's outside our own comfort zone.

- It's easier to feel empathy for people we see as like us or part of our social network. When students see ways that we are all connected, they will have an increased sense of responsibility for each other.

- a good friend
- someone who is less popular than you are
- someone who is very popular
- someone you don't know who is being teased
- someone you don't like
- someone who has hurt your feelings in the past
- someone who is the same age as you
- someone who is five years older than you
- someone who is five years younger than you
- someone you don't see very often
- someone famous who experienced a tragedy
- someone from another state whose house was destroyed by a tornado
- a neighbor
- victims of war in another country
- someone who looks like you
- someone who looks different from you (different race, gender, or ethnicity)

7. Have students return to the large circle and discuss their observations.

Discussion Questions (20 minutes)

1. **Why do you think it's easier to feel empathy for someone we like versus someone we don't like—or someone who may have hurt us in the past?**
2. **How does empathy help control our words and actions toward others?**
3. **What role does empathy play in bullying situations?** (Students engaged in bullying probably lack empathy. Bystanders may have high or low levels of empathy.)
4. **How can we show empathy toward those who are being bullied? What would be an impact of either high or low levels of empathy for the person being bullied from bystanders?**

Wrap-Up

1. **Empathy is a powerful tool for learning to get along with others. Feeling and showing empathy is especially important in helping to stop bullying. It takes careful listening and observation to learn to see things from someone else's point of view.**

Dig Deeper

- Many people who bully can be quite good at identifying how others feel (such as knowing what "pushes someone's buttons"). But the fact that they either do not care if their behavior hurts someone's feelings or may even enjoy hurting others shows a lack of empathy.

- A lack of empathy allows one person to exploit or bully another without remorse.

Showing empathy may also take a lot of courage, especially when people's lives or experiences are very different from our own. I want to challenge each of you to think of ways you can show empathy to someone this week. We'll report back at the beginning of our next class meeting.

2. Encourage additional questions and comments.

Curriculum Connections

Vocabulary: *compassion, empathy, perspective-taking, sympathy*

Social Studies: Have students research acts of mercy/empathy in history and current events.

English: Suggest that students write journal entries for the following:

- two examples of empathetic responses that would be meaningful to you
- a time when someone showed empathy toward you
- a time when you missed an important opportunity to show empathy toward another

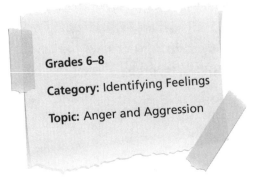

Grades 6–8

Category: Identifying Feelings

Topic: Anger and Aggression

Handling Anger in Healthy Ways

Background

As students go through major physical and hormonal changes, they may find it challenging to regulate and interpret strong emotions, including anger. Students can benefit from opportunities to understand emotions and to learn positive ways to channel anger. Because these years are often filled with emotional stress, it is important that adults establish close connections with students and be aware when they need additional emotional support.

Learner Outcomes

By the end of this session, students will be able to
- identify situations that trigger anger (and describe its physical manifestations)
- identify personal triggers for anger
- describe personal strategies for channeling their anger in positive ways

Materials Needed

- Chalkboard and chalk or dry erase board and markers

Preparation Needed

None

Class Meeting Outline

Opening Activity (10 minutes)

1. **Everyone gets angry sometimes. In your opinion, is anger a positive or negative emotion? Are there ever situations where anger is appropriate? When?** Write students' ideas on the board. Examples of situations where showing anger is appropriate include responding to injustice, inequity, or cruelty.

2. **It's not always easy to interpret what people are feeling. What are some signs you can see or hear that indicate a person is angry?**

3. **What are words that describe shades or types of anger?** (Examples include *annoyed, furious, irritated, exasperated, hostile, violent, frustrated,* and *jealous.*)

4. Divide the students up into pairs. (See pages 13–14 for ideas and strategies for grouping students.) **With your partner, discuss one thing that annoys or irritates you or causes mild anger, and then one thing that really makes you furious or very angry. How do you generally express these different levels of anger? Give an example of something you do to control your anger, let off steam, or calm down.**

5. Give pairs a few minutes to discuss, and then have them return to the large circle.

Dig Deeper

While anger is a natural response to injustice, it is never an excuse for retaliatory behavior that physically hurts others. Help students find peaceful ways to deal with their anger. Students should know that most bullying is not done by students out of anger. See page 23 in the Teacher Guide for information about typical motives for bullying.

Discussion Questions (25 minutes)

1. **What are some examples of ways you and your partner typically respond when angry?**

2. **What do you and your partner have in common in terms of what triggers angry feelings and how you express those feelings? What differences do you have?**

3. **What things might trigger anger for different people?** Write this list of triggers on the board.

4. **Are there times when your response makes things worse for you? Are there times when your response makes things better for you?**

5. **What patterns do you see? Are there differences between boys and girls and the way they handle anger?**

6. **What other factors affect the way people respond and react to anger?** (Answers might include upbringing, culture, temperament, situation, or the person you are with.)

   - **Do you think our society sets different standards for different people when it comes to showing anger? For example, is it more acceptable for some people to show anger than others?**
   - **What are some stereotypes about displays of anger?** (Women express less anger than men, men get angry faster, women may be less violent than men in their response to anger.)

7. **How can we tell the difference between healthy and unhealthy anger?**

   - **What are some examples of unhealthy ways of dealing with anger?** (Answers might include keeping feelings bottled up inside, turning anger inside on yourself, doing things to hurt yourself, using alcohol or other drugs to numb the feelings, or acting out.) List responses on the board.
   - **What are some healthy ways to express or release anger?** (Answers might include counting to ten, walking away, talking it through, or getting exercise.) List responses on the board.

8. **We've been talking about recognizing and dealing with anger within ourselves. Let's consider situations where we come up against anger in others. When we encounter angry people, it can be difficult to know what responses might be most appropriate or productive. Sometimes actions can even make things worse.**

   - **How do you decide how to deal with angry people?**
   - **Are some choices more likely to be effective than others?**

9. Discuss anger as it relates directly to bullying:

   - **What role do you think anger plays in bullying situations?** Discuss from the perspective of the person who bullies, the bystander, and the person being bullied.
   - **What are healthy ways for students who are bullied to deal with their anger?**
   - **What are examples of ways bystanders can use their anger to motivate change in a positive way?**

Wrap-Up

1. **Anger is a normal human response that can be positive if channeled in a healthy way. Whenever you get angry, try using a healthy response to handle it. If you see bullying, it would be natural to feel anger. If you feel comfortable, try to intervene in a positive and healthy way.**

2. Encourage additional questions and comments.

Curriculum Connections

Vocabulary: *ambiguous, angry, annoyed, constructive, destructive, escalate, exasperated, furious, hostile, impulses, inequity, injustice, jealous, regulate, stereotypes, violent*

Social Studies/English:

- Have students write or discuss answers to the following: If humans never felt or expressed anger, how would the world be different? What would be better? What would be worse? Ask students to give examples from history or literature to support their point of view.

- Point out that history is full of examples of people who were motivated by anger to take action. Have students research events that show positive anger (civil disobedience, social activism) and negative anger (riots, terrorism). As appropriate, draw on examples of anger that affect the students' own lives and community.

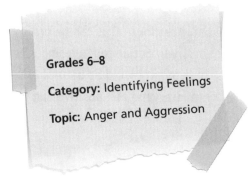

Grades 6–8

Category: Identifying Feelings

Topic: Anger and Aggression

Assertive or Aggressive? What's the Difference?

Background

Negotiating the line between assertive and aggressive behavior can be challenging for all of us. But it's particularly difficult for young people, whose actions and decision-making are often governed by emotions and impulse. In a society that tends to reward aggression and power-based interactions, students get very mixed messages about what behavior is acceptable. Aggression in bullying situations is not just physical; it may take many forms. We want students to be appropriately assertive in their interactions, but we also want them to recognize when behaviors cross the line to become aggressive, especially in regard to bullying situations. Responding to aggression with more aggression can cause bullying to escalate. Students need opportunities to practice assertive responses to aggressive bullying behavior.

Learner Outcomes

By the end of this session, students will be able to

- identify differences between assertive and aggressive behavior in bullying situations
- describe how assertiveness is a positive, healthy response to anger, and aggression is usually a negative, unhealthy response to anger
- demonstrate using assertive behaviors
- recognize that it takes courage to respond assertively to aggression and bullying and that being assertive is not the same as being without fear

Materials Needed

- Bullying Scenarios on page 44

Preparation Needed

- Copy the handout and cut apart the scenarios. Make enough copies so each group of three to four students has one scenario.

Class Meeting Outline

Opening Activity (20 minutes)

1. **We've discussed ways that we can respond positively and negatively when we're angry. Let's quickly review some of the positive ways.**

2. Review the terms "assertive" and "aggressive." Ask students to explain the difference between the two when it comes to bullying situations. (For example, assertive behavior seeks to stop aggression whereas an aggressive response can sometimes escalate aggression; being assertive allows you to be firm but positive.) Ask students to give examples of assertive and aggressive behavior in regard to bullying situations. (When you're assertive, you speak up for yourself, make good eye contact, find solutions, and consider others' feelings. When you're aggressive, you don't think about the feelings of others.)

3. **Being assertive is a skill we can use in many areas of our lives. It can help us make better choices and get better results when we're angry. What are some examples of assertive choices you can make when you see or hear something that you feel is wrong?**

4. **What can make being assertive more difficult or challenging?** (Answers might include the situation, your own personality, personal experiences, and whether you feel unsure or afraid.)

5. **Each of us has a personality that affects how naturally assertive we are. We all need to practice ways of acting assertive to gain confidence in our abilities to stand up for ourselves and others. Today, we're going to practice being assertive in different situations.**

6. Review or practice assertive body language and voice by using one of the scenarios as an example. Read the scenario and have the students

brainstorm an example of an assertive response and an example of an aggressive response. Discuss briefly.

7. Divide the class into groups of three or four students. (See pages 13–14 for ideas and strategies for grouping students.) Each group should designate a member as the Student Who Bullies, the Student Who Is Bullied, and the Bystanders.

   a. Give each group a scenario strip and have them "start the action" after the bullying incident, with the bystander(s) showing assertive behavior to address the bullying.

   b. Have the students practice three times—switching roles each time and trying out as many different assertive strategies as possible.

8. Have the groups return to the large circle and process the activity.

Discussion Questions (20 minutes)

1. **What were some things you observed? How did it feel being assertive? How was it different standing alone rather than with someone as backup?**

2. **When you were in the bullying role, how did it feel having another student approach you in an assertive way? How might this help stop bullying?**

3. **When you were in the bullied role, how did it feel when the bystander stood up for you?**

4. **What are some assertive "one-liners" that might be effective bystander statements to make to students who are bullying?** Have students create a list. (Some ideas include "Leave him/her alone," "Don't talk to him/her that way," "Be fair," or "That wasn't funny.") A student volunteer may compile the list, print it, and distribute it to the class. If the school uses an assignment notebook, students may also copy this list into their notebooks for future reference.

5. **What are examples of situations where it would be challenging to be assertive without being mean?**

6. **Why do you think the same strategies don't work in every situation?**

7. **Why do you think that responding to bullying with aggressive behavior or more bullying might escalate the problem?**

8. **What are examples where responding to bullying assertively takes more courage than responding aggressively, or not responding at all?**

9. **What if you don't feel comfortable or safe stepping in to stop bullying? Are there ways to respond assertively to bullying *after* it happens?** Have students create a list. (Some examples include talk with a teacher or other adult at school later; speak to the bullied student later to let him/her know you feel bad about what happened; invite the bullied student to do something with you; speak with the bullying student later and say that you don't think what happened was right.) A student volunteer may compile the list, print it, and distribute it to the class. If the school uses an assignment notebook, students may also copy this list into their notebooks for future reference.

10. **If a bystander or if a bullied student responds to bullying with assertive behavior, is it still necessary to tell an adult? Why or why not?**

Wrap-Up

1. **It takes courage to counter bullying with assertive behavior. Being assertive is easier and more effective when we stand up together, rather than alone. You may be unsure whether your response has helped, but don't give up! Our collective effort (adults and students) can create changes so everyone feels safer and more welcome in our school. We'll continue to practice different techniques and share ideas. Let's review these techniques in a few weeks to see how being assertive is working.** (Make a note to follow up!)

2. Encourage additional questions and comments.

Curriculum Connections

Vocabulary: *aggression, aggressive, assertive, collective, de-escalation, violence*

Science: Have students list physical responses to being fearful (racing heart, dry throat, sweaty palms, and tensed body). Discuss how these responses help or hinder us in responding to dangerous or scary situations.

English: Have students look in the media (TV, videos, books, movies, newspapers) for examples of people choosing assertive behavior over aggressive behavior. Have them share their examples with the class and critique whether the choices were effective, realistic, and safe.

Bullying Scenarios

Instructions: Copy the cards and cut them apart. Give each group one scenario.

✂

An older student walks up to your best friend, grabs your friend's homework, crumples it, and then throws it on the floor.

On the way to your first class of the day, you and a friend have to walk by a group of students who have repeatedly attempted to push, trip, or otherwise make fun of your friend.

A group of popular girls frequently point and laugh when they see Jennie, a girl in special education, coming down the hall. Jennie has told you that she's found mean notes on her locker. You think the girls are responsible.

A student whose locker is a few lockers down from yours is frequently bullied by a student whose locker is a little further down the row. You notice the bullying is getting worse.

When attending a basketball game, you notice that some other kids in the bleachers are throwing popcorn at a couple of younger students nearby and calling them names.

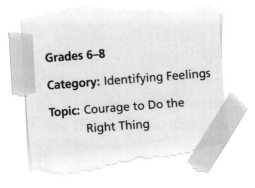

Grades 6–8

Category: Identifying Feelings

Topic: Courage to Do the
Right Thing

Courage

Background

It takes courage even for adults to respond to bullying, and to know what the best options would be. For students, it may seem easier to do nothing than to do what they think is right, especially because of the role that peer pressure plays in "going along with the crowd." Adults can help change this pattern and shift student attitudes and behavior so that doing the right thing becomes an acceptable part of school culture, and so that students who are proactive bystanders feel supported and confident rather than isolated or ridiculed. This class meeting should be conducted after the class meeting on assertiveness.

Learner Outcomes

By the end of this session, students will be able to

- recognize and describe opportunities to show courage and to respond to bullying
- demonstrate a range of options for responding to bullying situations courageously

Materials Needed

- Paper and pencils
- Chalkboard and chalk or dry erase board and markers
- How Much Courage? handout on page 49

Preparation Needed

- Make sure each student has paper and a pencil.
- Create a grid on the board like the one on page 49.
- Select four items from the following list of social dilemmas.
  - ○ starting a new school midyear
  - ○ standing up to someone who bullies you
  - ○ not cheating on a difficult test when you get the perfect opportunity
  - ○ making your first dive from the high board at the pool
  - ○ admitting you've been bullying someone
  - ○ befriending someone who is seen as an outcast and very unpopular
  - ○ going out for a team sport you're not very good at playing
  - ○ taking the lead in the school musical
  - ○ being seen in out-of-date, ugly clothes
  - ○ standing up for someone who is bullied
  - ○ giving up your seat to someone on a bus
  - ○ smiling at someone who seems to be in a bad mood
  - ○ helping someone who intimidates you with homework
  - ○ picking up some trash that someone else dropped
- Copy the handout, one per student.

Class Meeting Outline

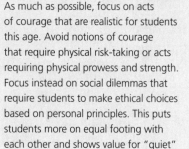

Teacher Tip

As much as possible, focus on acts of courage that are realistic for students this age. Avoid notions of courage that require physical risk-taking or acts requiring physical prowess and strength. Focus instead on social dilemmas that require students to make ethical choices based on personal principles. This puts students more on equal footing with each other and shows value for "quiet" or "everyday" acts of courage that often go unnoticed.

Opening Activity (10 minutes)

1. **Having courage doesn't mean having no fear. Many people who stand up for what they believe in feel afraid, but courage helps them overcome their fear or to act in spite of it.**

2. **We tend to think about courage as it relates to saving someone's life or taking big physical risks, but most acts of courage happen on a smaller scale in everyday life. We all have the power to show courage by standing up for our principles and doing the right thing, even if it's not a popular choice. These small acts of courage add up.**

3. **Today's activity will give you a chance to indicate how much courage you think would be needed in certain social situations.** Distribute the handout. Read each social dilemma you have selected. For each, ask students to raise their hands to indicate whether they think that situation would take no courage, some courage, or a lot of courage. Record the number of votes for each category on the grid you have prepared. Encourage students to do the same on their handout.

4. Have students look at the grid and discuss their observations.

Discussion Questions (20 minutes)

1. **What pattern, if any, do you notice? What situations did many of you feel required greater amounts of courage? Did these situations have anything in common? What factors influenced how much courage you felt it would take for you to stand up for your principles and do the right thing?**

2. **Describe a social situation where you have acted courageously.**

3. **What factors make it hard for students your age to stand up for their principles? to show courage in social situations? to go against the crowd? What might make you compromise or go against your personal principles?**

4. **What are times you might need courage to stand up for people or issues here at this school?**

5. **Does it take more courage to do what is right in a social situation or to protest against something that you think is unfair or unjust?**

6. **Whom do you admire for having the courage to do the right thing?**

7. **Do you think our society has different standards or expectations for men and women about what it means to be courageous?** Discuss differences in standards and how that might create or reinforce negative stereotypes or unhealthy views. **How do those stereotypes affect choices made by students your age?**

8. **What are some ways you can show courage in your everyday lives? in bullying situations?**

Teacher Tip

Use this class meeting to highlight an everyday hero from your school or town—an average person who acted courageously by standing up for something he or she believed in.

Wrap-Up

1. **Courage can help us make the right choices and do the right thing, even when it's unpopular to go against the crowd. It takes courage to keep trying to make things better, especially when we are not initially successful or are faced with roadblocks. Most of us are never called on to act as heroes in the traditional sense (as lifesavers), but small acts of courage add up.**

   We can all be courageous and we can be heroes through positive choices and everyday acts that protect and help others. I want to challenge each of you over the next week or so to choose to be courageous by helping out someone here at school. We'll start our next class meeting sharing some of your experiences, and how things turned out. (Make a note to follow up!)

2. Encourage additional questions and comments.

Curriculum Connections

Vocabulary: *courage, dilemmas, ethics, heroes, persevere, persist, principles*

English: Suggest the following for journal writing:

- Create a statement about your personal principles or ethics, what you believe about doing the right thing. How do you decide to make ethical or just choices?

- Write about a time when you wish you would have acted more courageously. Describe what you wish you would have said or done.

Social Studies/History/Civics: Have students research and write about someone in history, your community, or their family who demonstrated "quiet acts of courage." Encourage them to look for individuals who stood up for their principles, even when it was unpopular or risky to do so.

Media Studies: Ask students to look for examples in the media of unhealthy stereotypes about courage.

How Much Courage?

Instructions: For each situation, write down the number of students who voted for "a lot of courage," "some courage," and "no courage."

	A lot of courage	Some courage	No courage
Situation #1			
Situation #2			
Situation #3			
Situation #4			

Category 3

Communication

(Six class meetings)

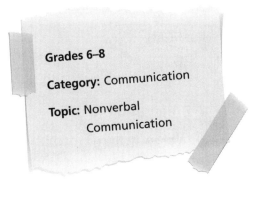

Grades 6–8

Category: Communication

Topic: Nonverbal Communication

The Masks We Wear

Background

Everyone disguises their true feelings, thoughts, and personality at some time or another. Learning when and where it is safe and appropriate to reveal our true feelings is an important coping skill. Middle school students are exploring who they are, and they often "try on" different traits as one way of learning about their identities. Developmentally, they are torn between wanting to assert their individuality and wanting to blend in with peers. Adults can facilitate healthy emotional development by providing vocabulary to identify and label feelings, teaching skills that nurture true friendships, and helping students practice appropriate ways to protect themselves emotionally. In addition, students this age continue to need practice reading body language and nonverbal cues, seeing situations from another's perspective, and identifying factors that motivate behavior.

Learner Outcomes

By the end of this session, students will be able to

- discuss different ways people express the same emotion
- describe situations that limit students' abilities to show their true feelings or "true selves" at school or in social situations with peers
- identify safe or appropriate ways to mask feelings or personal information
- identify ways in which masking feelings can have positive and negative effects

Materials Needed

- Index cards (two per student)
- Markers

Preparation Needed

- You may wish to wear a mask to introduce this activity.
- Write a different emotion vocabulary word on each index card. Select from the following list and add others as appropriate for your age group: afraid, angry, confused, content, depressed, detached, disappointed/dejected, ecstatic, embarrassed/mortified, enthused, envious, excited, frustrated, furious, guarded, happy, hopeful, humiliated, jealous, ruthless, surprised, sympathetic, tentative, thrilled, and uncertain. Be sure to create enough so each student will have two cards for the activity. Some of these words can be repeated.

Class Meeting Outline

Opening Activity (10 minutes)

1. **How many of you have dressed up in a costume or worn a mask that covered all or part of your face for Halloween or a school play or something like that?** Have students respond by raising their hands.

2. **When you were in costume, did you feel your real identity was concealed or altered? How many of you felt the costume allowed you to feel or act in ways that you normally wouldn't? Did being "in character" allow you to express feelings or a personality of your character? If so, how did it feel? Did you behave the same or differently than you usually do?** Encourage students to describe how they felt or acted when their real self was hidden.

3. **What does it mean to say "His face was like a mask" or "She's masking her feelings"?**

4. **We're going to try a game to practice recognizing different emotions.** Divide students into teams of three or four, giving each team a set of six to eight emotion vocabulary cards. (See pages 13–14 for ideas and

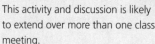

Teacher Tip

This activity and discussion is likely to extend over more than one class meeting.

strategies for grouping students.) Explain that students will take turns drawing a card and then pantomiming the emotion on the card. Team members will try to guess the emotion. They should note how facial expressions or body language tip them off. Give time for each person to go at least once—preferably twice with different emotions each time.

5. Gather teams back together in a large circle for discussion.

Discussion Questions (15 minutes)

1. **What did you notice about your teammates' facial expressions or body language? Was it easy or difficult to identify the emotions?**

2. **Which emotions were the easiest for you to identify? Which were the hardest?**

3. **What are situations where people might choose to mask their true feelings? What reasons could students at school have for hiding or masking their emotions?**

4. **When might hiding one's emotions be a good idea?** (Answers might include as a coping mechanism, for protection, to keep from being embarrassed, to be tactful.)

5. **Why might it not be a good idea to hide your feelings?** (Holding negative emotions inside can be unhealthy. Keeping emotions bottled up makes you lonely, keeps you from being able to connect with others, and might keep you from getting help or support for a problem. People never get to see the real you. You could seem dishonest or manipulative.)

Dig Deeper

Many students (and adults) have difficulty reading social cues. It's important to provide students with opportunities to practice recognizing these cues at other times, such as during other class discussions, and not just at these class meetings.

6. **Most of us try to put our best selves forward for others. What do you think most kids at school are trying to show about themselves? Why?**

7. **Do you show the same mask or emotions to your close friends and family as you do with people you don't know that well at school? Why or why not?**

8. **Which is easier: masking your emotions when talking to someone in person or masking your emotions when talking to someone using technology such as cell phones, email, or instant messaging? Why do you think that is?**

9. **Have you ever been misunderstood in an email or a text message because someone couldn't see your face or hear your voice? How did you handle that or try to correct the misunderstanding? What can you**

do to prevent this kind of misunderstanding and communicate what you really mean?

10. **How can written words take on different meanings when we send them to others?**

11. **What can you do to let the person on the other end of the email, text message, or instant messaging conversation know what you really mean?**

Wrap-Up

1. **We all mask our true feelings at times. Sometimes that can help protect us, but sometimes it can interfere with our ability to make friends. Being able to read and understand facial expressions and body language can give us important information about what people are feeling. Being aware of nonverbal cues can also help protect us from harm. We'll revisit some of these ideas because they can help us deal with bullying.**

2. Encourage additional questions and comments.

Curriculum Connections

Vocabulary: *alter, body language, conceal, content, cues, depressed, disappointed/dejected, ecstatic, embarrassed/mortified, envious, excited, frustrated, furious, humiliated, identity, mask, nonverbal communication, pretense, tentative, uncertain* (add all emotions used on cards)

English: Have students write about a time when they masked their emotions. Or have them write about a character in age-appropriate literature who did so. Encourage students to include the reason for masking emotions, the pros and cons of doing so, the feelings it created for them or the character, and the effect those actions had on others.

Science: Explore the role body language or nonverbal cues play in animal and human behavior. How do animals respond to cues? Encourage students to observe human body language in public settings such as supermarkets and bus stops.

Art: Have students make collages showing different emotions.

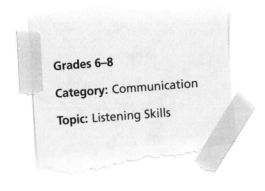

Grades 6–8

Category: Communication

Topic: Listening Skills

Paying Attention to Clues

Background

By the middle school years, many students have experienced some sort of bullying—and some have been bullied for a year or more. While younger students often report bullying to adults, older students are less likely to do so because they may feel embarrassed or lack confidence in adults' responses. Although they are somewhat more likely to tell their peers, many students silently endure the pain and humiliation of bullying, often turning those feelings inward. This class meeting helps raise awareness and empathy so that students may detect clues that classmates may need help, and allows them to brainstorm ways they might intervene and provide social support in the aftermath of bullying. This class meeting may last two sessions if your class needs to be introduced to the concept of "body language."

Learner Outcomes

By the end of this session, students will be able to
- describe both obvious and more subtle signs of bullying
- identify questions students can use when they suspect a student is being bullied
- identify active listening skills to show that they are really listening
- explain why individual responsibility extends to all peers, not just friends

Materials Needed

- Scenarios for Paying Attention to Clues on page 59
- Chalkboard and chalk or dry erase board and markers

Preparation Needed

- Make copies of the handout for each student.
- Write these questions on the board:
  - What clues in a classmate's body language let you know that something is wrong?
  - What verbal clues or words let you know that something is wrong?
  - What clues might the person be giving that he or she is masking hurt emotions?
  - What are some questions you can ask to help him or her?
- Make sure you have enough space so groups have some distance and privacy from each other.

Class Meeting Outline

Opening Activity (15 minutes)

1. Break the class into groups of three or four students. (See pages 13–14 for ideas and strategies for grouping students.) Have each group begin by discussing the "icebreaker" question: **How can you tell when someone is being bullied?**
2. Distribute copies of the handout. Assign one scenario to each group. The scenarios may be assigned to more than one group.
3. Ask students to first read their scenario to themselves. Students will then decide who will act out the role of the main character and who will act out the roles of the friends or bystanders. The friends or bystanders will ask questions to find out what is troubling the main character. Remind groups to model their questions around those listed on the board.
4. Allow time for the group role-plays. Then have the students return to the large circle for discussion.

Teacher Tip

Invite students to create a list for parents of signs that their child may be the target of bullying.

Discussion Questions (20 minutes)

1. **How can you tell if someone is being bullied? What are some obvious clues?** Write the heading Obvious Clues of Bullying and student responses on the board. (Responses might include bruises or lacerations, visible fear, witnessing someone being bullied, damaged personal property, and notes or derogatory graffiti on a student's locker.)

2. **What are some more subtle clues that someone is being bullied?** Write the heading Subtle Clues of Bullying and student responses on the board. (Responses might include frequent absences from school, increased physical illnesses, signs of stress, falling grades, low appetite, loss of interest in regular activities, avoiding hallways or normal routes home, body language clues such as avoiding eye contact or head down, tired appearance, increased anxiety, and lack of friends.)

3. **How can you pay attention to both the obvious and the subtle clues to know if something is wrong or someone might be being bullied?**

4. **What are some specific questions you could ask a classmate or friend if you suspect he or she is being bullied?** Write the questions on the board as students discuss.

5. **How can you let this classmate know that you are really listening to him or her?** (Responses may include such active listening skills as maintaining eye contact, asking clarifying questions, and restating what the person said.) If students are unfamiliar with active listening techniques, demonstrate them with a volunteer.

6. **How can you empathize with a classmate about being bullied even if you have never experienced it?**

7. **If you were being bullied and hadn't opened up about it to anyone, would you want someone to keep asking you what was wrong? Why or why not? What reasons might students have to tell no one?**

8. **Do you think repeated bullying might change someone's personality? If so, how?**

9. **Should you care about the fate of someone who is not your friend? Why or why not? What responsibility do you have to strangers in your school if you find out one of them is being bullied?**

10. **Imagine you are creating a list of safe adults that you or others could talk to if you or they had been bullied. What kinds of people would be on the list?**

Wrap-Up

1. **When someone has a secret he or she feels is shameful, it can be difficult to find the courage to tell someone. Be mindful of the obvious and subtle signs that someone in your school is being bullied, and seek those individuals out to offer your support, even if it is not initially welcomed.**

2. Encourage additional questions and comments.

Curriculum Connections

Vocabulary: *active listening skills, clues, courage, empathy, fate, offensive, personality, subtle*

Health: Discuss the physical and emotional consequences of being targeted for bullying. These include headaches and stomachaches, anxiety and depression, tiredness and inability to sleep, increased isolation, loss of focus on schoolwork, and less or no interest in activities once found enjoyable.

Art: Have students draw what a person's body language may look like when being bullied, and also the body language of a person bullying others. This could also be done using sculpture.

Science: Explore with students what is known about how the body is affected by stress and being bullied. Explore what is known about developmental behaviors of those who bully others.

Scenarios for Paying Attention to Clues

1. A group of popular students started calling you an offensive name. Now other students are referring to you by that same name—even outside of school and around your neighborhood.

2. A few kids have pushed or tripped you when you walk down the hall or are at your locker or when you try to find a seat at lunch.

3. For several weeks the group of kids you used to eat with makes it clear that there is no room for you at the table. You often have a hard time finding a seat with other kids, so you eat alone.

4. You've put on some weight recently. Kids have been making comments about how you look. They call you names like "fatso" and "big deal" whenever you walk down the hall. You are crushed. Even your so-called friends laugh along.

5. Someone created a "hot or not" Web site where students can rate whether or not their peers are good looking. Some of the comments on the "not" list are very derogatory and cruel. You find your name on the "not" list, along with some of the worst comments on the site.

6. Your friends suddenly start ignoring your IMs after school and on the weekends. You have no idea why. You've asked, and no one will respond to your questions. What's worse, they've started ignoring you at school as well. You feel horrible and very left out.

7. You find out that there is a rumor going around school about you that is completely untrue. This rumor is ruining your reputation, and you have no idea who started it or why. You start to make up excuses to stay home from school.

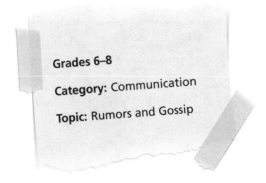

Grades 6–8

Category: Communication

Topic: Rumors and Gossip

Spreading Rumors and Gossip

Background

Spreading gossip and rumors about others is a common form of bullying among students in middle school. As students perfect their verbal communication skills and as social alliances shift, they learn that words can be powerful tools in negotiating social situations and in intimidating and isolating peers. Gossip and rumors are especially frustrating because the source may be unidentified, and hurtful communication can spread widely and quickly. Students need clear messages from adults that bullying by spreading hurtful rumors, gossip, private personal information, or lies is something that individuals can choose to stop. This class meeting is designed to remind students that once a rumor, a lie, or gossip is repeated, it never really goes away.

Learner Outcomes

By the end of this session, students will be able to
- identify forms of rumor-spreading and gossip that are used at school
- discuss the difficulty in stopping rumors and destructive gossip
- identify possible options for responding to rumors and gossip

Materials Needed

- Spreading Rumors and Gossip: A Fable on page 64

Preparation Needed

- Become familiar with the fable provided in the handout or use age-appropriate literature that depicts gossip or spreading rumors (examples include *Stargirl* by Jerry Spinelli and *Tangerine* by Edward Bloor).
- Make copies of the handout for each student.

Class Meeting Outline

Opening Activity (5 minutes)

1. **Today we are going to talk about verbal bullying or using words to hurt others. One type of verbal bullying is spreading gossip and rumors.**
2. Distribute copies of the handout, and read the fable to the class. Alternatively, ask students to read selected passages from age-appropriate literature.
3. Explain that a fable is a story that teaches a lesson. Ask students to restate the lesson of this fable. (Gossip and rumors spread quickly and can't be taken back once spoken.) Then continue with a general discussion of gossip and rumors.

Teacher Tips

- If possible, dedicate two or three class meetings to the topic of spreading rumors and gossip to allow students time to explore this very relevant and complex topic.

- Other resources for stories about rumors and gossip include *Spinning Tales, Weaving Hope: Stories, Storytelling and Activities for Peace, Justice and the Environment* by Ed Brody, Jay Goldspinner, and Katie Green; and *Wisdom Tales from Around the World* by Heather Forest.

Discussion Questions (15 minutes)

1. **What are some examples of gossip or rumors that you have heard?** Caution students not to use names.
2. **What are the different ways that people can spread a rumor or gossip about someone?**
3. **Do rumors and gossip only involve untruths? Or can they involve truths that people don't want shared?**
4. **Why do you think students gossip and spread rumors about others?**
5. **Some people say girls gossip more often than boys. Do you agree? Why or why not?** (Research shows that boys as well as girls engage in spreading rumors and gossip and relational aggression. *Relational aggression* is indirect bullying that causes harm through and to relationships.)
6. **Being physically bullied and being bullied verbally are both painful experiences for those who are targeted. Is experiencing one kind of**

bullying worse than the other? Why or why not? (Research shows that both kinds of bullying are equally harmful.)

7. **How might gossiping about someone affect his or her life?** (Those targeted can lose their friends, their reputation, and their self-esteem and confidence. Some teens have become physically ill or have become anxious or depressed. Some have dropped out of school because of private information or lies told about them by their peers.)

8. **How might those who spread the rumors or gossip be affected?** (They may lose the trust of other people or become known as troublemakers. This behavior can become self-destructive.)

9. **Does it really matter who starts rumors or gossip if there are a number of people who repeat it? Is the person who started the rumor more to blame or more guilty than those who pass it along? Why or why not?**

10. **What can you do if rumors are being spread about you?**

11. **If you hear a rumor or gossip being spread about someone, can you do anything to stop it? How difficult would that be?**

12. **What can you do to help others who have had gossip or false rumors spread about them?**

Teacher Tip

Students may want to discuss rumors and gossip encountered in emails, instant messaging, or chat rooms or on social networking sites. Consider dedicating one class meeting to face-to-face communications and another to cyber bullying.

Wrap-Up

1. **Rumors and gossip may seem like interesting or exciting talk, but thoughtless and carelessly spoken words can be extremely cruel weapons used to bully others. STOP if you believe what you've heard from another person is gossip. THINK about the consequences of repeating rumors or gossip.**

2. Encourage additional questions and comments.

Curriculum Connections

Vocabulary: *defamation of character, gossip, lies, relational aggression, rumors*

English: Have students write a short story about teens who spread gossip or rumors about someone. They should show how the individual was hurt and how the gossip made the person feel. The students could also write about a character from fiction who was the target of gossip.

Math/Social Studies: Have students examine how pervasive rumors and gossiping behaviors are in their school. Ask them to observe and tally (over a two-day period) the number of times they hear a rumor or observe gossiping by students. (Remind students not to repeat the gossip!) They might keep track of information such as different topics of gossip, differences between boys and girls, or places within the school where they hear the rumors or gossip. Have students compile and chart the results and report on their findings.

Social Studies: Have students look at ways gossip and rumors have played a role in or affected events in history (for example, cold war diplomacy, decisions to go to war, spy rings, military coups, Rosenberg trials, McCarthyism, or U.S. presidential elections).

Art: Have students create posters suggesting ways to deal with verbal bullying. Display their "words of wisdom" posters in the classroom or key areas of the school where gossip and rumors are most likely to occur.

Music: Students may write new words to existing tunes, or write their own songs about gossip or rumors.

Spreading Rumors and Gossip: A Fable

Gossip

There was a man who gossiped constantly, always telling stories about his neighbors, even if he didn't know them very well, and the stories weren't always true. Wanting to change, he visited one of the wise farmers in his community for advice. The farmer instructed the man to buy a fresh chicken at the local market and bring it back to him as quickly as possible, plucking every single feather off the chicken as he ran. Not one feather was to remain. The man did as he was told, plucking as he ran, throwing feathers every which way until not a feather remained on that poor chicken. He handed the bare chicken over to the farmer, glad his task was completed. The farmer then asked the man to go back and gather the feathers he had plucked and bring them ALL back to him so they could be put back where they belonged. The man protested that this was impossible as he hadn't watched where he had thrown the feathers, and the wind must have carried those feathers in every direction. He said, "I'll never be able to find them all!" The farmer replied, "That's true. And that's how it is with gossip. One rumor can fly to many corners, and how could you ever retrieve it? It is better not to spread gossip in the first place!"

Adapted from *Spinning Tales, Weaving Hope: Stories, Storytelling and Activities for Peace, Justice and the Environment* by Ed Brody, Jay Goldspinner, and Katie Green (Gabriola, BC: New Society Publishers, 2002).

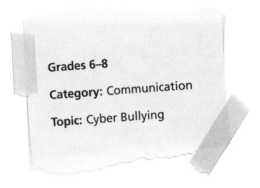

Grades 6–8

Category: Communication

Topic: Cyber Bullying

A Brief Overview of Cyber Bullying

Background

Computers, cell phones, and other electronic devices allow students to spread gossip and rumors and manipulate relationships with broader access and speed than "traditional" forms of bullying. In addition, students often feel a greater sense of anonymity when they use these tools to bully others, and they may also feel less responsibility for the harm they cause. Adults need to understand that, even when conducted outside of school or off school grounds, this behavior can have profound effects on student interaction and performance in school. Adults should familiarize themselves with social networking sites, text messaging, blogs, and other forms of widely used cyber communications. This will help them to understand the impact and scope of cyber bullying and prepare them to prevent and respond to it.

Learner Outcomes

By the end of this session, students will be able to
- define cyber bullying and identify ways it is used
- describe ways that cyber bullying is harmful
- identify strategies to deal with cyber bullying in a variety of roles (including as participant, recipient, and/or bystander)
- describe controls and consequences the school has in place to prevent cyber bullying

Materials Needed

- Paper and pencils
- Chalkboard and chalk or dry erase board and markers
- *Optional:* Copies of online news stories involving cyber bullying and youth in grades 6–12

Preparation Needed

- Make sure each student has paper and a pencil.

Class Meeting Outline

Opening Activity (10 minutes)

1. Write the term "cyber bullying" on the board. Ask students if they know what this is. If you have found online news articles about cyber bullying, share these with the class. Otherwise, use these examples:
   - You emailed a friend with details about something that happened to you and asked this person not to share it with anyone else. The next day, you receive a forwarded email from someone else that contains the private information you sent to your friend. You find out that the email has been forwarded to almost everyone in your school.
   - Someone took an embarrassing picture of you with a cell phone and sent it to almost everyone in your class.

2. **Did you know that one in three teens who are online have experienced some sort of online harassment or cyber bullying?**[2]

3. Distribute paper and pencils. **On your own, list ways people can communicate in cyberspace.** (Students might list email, blogs, Web sites, instant messaging, cell phones, text messaging, chat rooms, and social networking sites.) **Next to each type of cyber communication write a way that it could become a tool for bullying.**

Dig Deeper

"About one-third (32 percent) of all teenagers who use the Internet say they have been targets of a range of annoying and potentially menacing online activities—such as receiving threatening messages; having their private emails or text messages forwarded without consent; having an embarrassing picture posted without permission; or having rumors about them spread online."[3]

4. Allow a few minutes for students to work individually. Then invite them to share their lists with the class. Write responses on the board.

Discussion Questions (20 minutes)

1. **How might it feel physically and emotionally to see a text or email message from someone who's bullying you? How might it feel to see that person in school?**

2. **Is there any difference in how you'd feel or react if a student makes fun of you in the hallway versus if the same student makes fun of you in an email? Why or why not?** (Students might note that the person could send the email to everyone in his or her address book. In turn, the email could get forwarded to everyone in the recipients' address books.)

3. **If you are cyber bullied at home by an anonymous person, how might that affect how you behave at school?** (Answers might include avoiding people at school, having physical symptoms of nervousness and fear, staying home sick more often, or feeling isolated.)

4. **How can you defend someone else who is being cyber bullied?** Suggest the following situations for discussion:

   - Your group of friends decides that you all should send a nasty email to someone in your class who said something bad about one of you.
   - You receive a text message with a link to a Web site that bashes a student at your school whom you don't particularly like.
   - You come across a MySpace or Facebook page that lists unpopular students at your school and says humiliating things about each of them.
   - Someone you know catches an embarrassing moment of someone else tripping and falling down the stairs at school and shares with you that he or she is planning on posting it on YouTube.

   (Answers might include posting positive messages on social networking Web sites and blogs, sending a "reply all" email

Teacher Tip

Consider using the Teacher Guide DVD scenario on cyber bullying called "Brenna in Homeroom" and accompanying discussion questions.

Teacher Tip

For more information on cyber bullying, talk to your certified *OBPP* trainer. You might also use Hazelden's *Cyber Bullying: A Prevention Curriculum for Grades 6–12* to supplement your school's program. Sessions in this curriculum are intended for use in class meetings. See www.hazelden.org/cyberbullying.

with a "knock it off" message to the sender, or emailing or text messaging a friendly word of encouragement to someone being cyber bullied.)

5. **Compared with traditional forms of bullying, it often is easier for a student to document cyber bullying. Look at the ways to communicate in cyberspace that we listed. How could a person document cyber bullying?** (Answers include saving and printing the emails, text messages, and IMs or copying and printing the screen shot of a derogatory Web site.)

6. **Do you think kids are reluctant to report cyber bullying that they've experienced or witnessed to adults like parents or teachers? Why or why not? What would make it more comfortable for kids to report cyber bullying?**

Wrap-Up

1. **Cyber bullying is a form of intimidation just as serious as traditional forms of bullying. At least the threats in cyber bullying are more easily documented, so if you or someone you know is targeted, save the evidence and get help. Remember to defend someone else who is being cyber bullied. Try to help in one of the ways we discussed.**

2. Encourage additional questions and comments.

Curriculum Connections

Vocabulary: *anonymous, cyber bullying, free speech, harassment, intimidation, slander*

Social Studies: Have students research the terms *free speech*, *slander*, and *libel*; laws about cyber bullying; Internet rights; or privacy/use policies on specific Web sites.

English or Art: Have students create a pamphlet about Internet safety and etiquette (often referred to as *netiquette*).

Drama or English: Have students suggest scenarios about cyber bullying and act them out. Use the role-plays to brainstorm solutions to this hurtful behavior. Ask students to focus on what to do if they get drawn into participating.

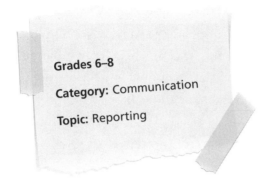

Grades 6–8

Category: Communication

Topic: Reporting

To Report or Not to Report?

Background

Students this age struggle with deciding whether or not to report bullying. Factors that come into the decision-making process include confusion about whether or not what they witnessed was really bullying, pressure from friends and others to stay quiet, not wanting to be seen as a "snitch" or as "tattling," fear of retaliation from the person(s) doing the bullying, and not knowing whom to tell. Adults should set the tone and create a safe atmosphere in which students feel comfortable reporting bullying incidents.

Learner Outcomes

By the end of this session, students will be able to
- identify reasons that make it difficult to report bullying
- identify factors that come into play when deciding how and when to "do the right thing"
- create an action plan about how to handle reporting

Materials Needed

- Three sheets of paper
- Dark marker
- Tape
- To Report or Not to Report? Scenarios on page 73

Preparation Needed

- Make three signs: Yes, No, and Maybe/Not Sure/It Depends.
- Post the signs around the classroom. Clear sufficient space by each sign for your entire class to crowd in if necessary.
- Read through the scenarios.

Class Meeting Outline

Opening Activity (5–10 minutes)

1. **The decision to report bullying is sometimes a very difficult one. You may not be sure that what you witnessed is really bullying. Pressure from friends and others, not wanting to be seen as a "snitch" or as a "tattletale," or fear of retaliation from the person doing the bullying are all factors that can affect your decision. And because of these factors, sometimes bullying goes unreported.**

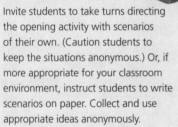

Teacher Tip

Invite students to take turns directing the opening activity with scenarios of their own. (Caution students to keep the situations anonymous.) Or, if more appropriate for your classroom environment, instruct students to write scenarios on paper. Collect and use appropriate ideas anonymously.

2. Indicate the three designated areas of the room. Explain to the group that you will read some scenarios. For each situation, they will need to decide Yes, they would report it; No, they would not report it; or Maybe/Not Sure/It Depends and then move to the corresponding area of the room.
3. Read the scenarios aloud. After each scenario, invite students to explain why they moved where they did.
4. Note those scenarios that students had the most difficulty with (the largest number of Maybe/Not Sure/It Depends) for the discussion.

Discussion Questions (25–30 minutes)

1. **How hard was it to decide if something was bullying or not? How hard was it to decide whether to report the situation?**
2. **Which scenarios seemed to be most controversial or difficult to decide what to do?**
3. **Were there any situations that you thought were bullying but would not report? Which ones? Why?**
4. **Were there any situations that you thought were bullying and would report? Which ones? Why?**

5. What are the risks of reporting for the bullied student? for the student(s) doing the reporting?

6. What are the benefits of reporting for the bullied student? for the student(s) doing the reporting? for the school as a whole?

7. Why are negative labels such as "snitch" or "rat" sometimes used to describe someone who does the right thing by reporting? What might it be like to be considered a "rat" by someone who bullies? How might the bullied person feel about you for reporting the bullying?

8. We each tend to view situations in a particular way, based on our experiences and personalities. Sometimes we see situations as more clear-cut or black or white; others may be less clear-cut or have more shades of gray. With bullying problems, what kinds of situations strike you as more clear-cut? What strike you as being less clear-cut?

Teacher Tip

Although many students are reluctant to report bullying, research indicates that bullying often does not stop without intervention.

9. How does what we've been discussing today relate to our school rule about reporting bullying?

Wrap-Up

1. Ask students to create a personal action plan for themselves about how and when they would report bullying, even when they are uncertain about the situation. Encourage them to think about what they would do if they feel uncertain whether something has crossed the line. What support systems can they rely on to help them put their plan into action?

2. For all of us (adults, too) it can be hard to decide whether or when to act—even when we know in our gut what is the right thing to do. It takes courage, and sometimes it seems that the negative consequences can be greater than the rewards, so we need to rely on each other for support. Put some of your good ideas into action over the next month, and we'll check back about how your plan is working.

Curriculum Connections

Vocabulary: *courage, reporting, snitch, whistleblowers*

Social Studies: Have students research and report on individuals who have been important whistle-blowers (such as Jeffrey Wigand who exposed the Big Tobacco scandal, Frederic Whitehurst who exposed irregularities at the FBI's crime lab, and Karen Silkwood who exposed safety problems in the nuclear industry). Encourage students to look for the person's traits and qualities and the positive and negative outcomes of the whistleblowing act.

English: Have students write a journal entry recalling a time when they took a stand for or against something. Were they the only one who took this position, or were they supported by others? How did it feel physically? emotionally?

To Report or Not to Report? Scenarios

Instructions: Read the following scenarios aloud to the group. Have the students decide if they would report it as bullying, not report it, or are not sure.

1. You get an email saying not to talk to a certain girl in school anymore and to forward the email to everyone you can.

2. A teacher repeatedly embarrasses one student at the chalkboard when the student is unable to do the requested math problem.

3. You saw someone secretly taking photos on a cell phone in the locker room after PE and laughing about them later.

4. Someone gets invited to play an online game but then gets teased after being beaten badly.

5. You heard that a kid at school was being beat up repeatedly on the way home from school, but you don't know for sure if it is true.

6. A new kid approaches a group of students and asks if he can hang out. A kid in the group says no and they turn away from the new kid.

7. You see two boys arguing in the parking lot, and one threatens to punch the other one.

8. You have a difficult time finding a seat on the school bus because all of the empty seats are "saved."

9. You raise your hand to answer questions in class. Later, in the hallway, a group of students makes fun of you for your class participation.

10. You know that all the kids in your class were invited to a party—except for one.

11. Someone set up a fake MySpace page and is posting false things about another student. The student is apparently unaware of what's going on.

Grades 6–8

Category: Communication

Topic: Problem Solving

Be Part of the Solution

Background

Students need lots of opportunities to problem-solve various ways of handling bullying situations. As their social experiences become more complex and peer relationships become more essential, students need positive reinforcement to make prosocial choices, and opportunities to think through pros and cons of potential choices. It is important to include opportunities for students to consider social supports (from students and adults) in handling bullying situations. Providing strong links to curriculum (especially through literature, current events, and history) can help students gain perspective about how "small acts of courage" can lead to broader social change.

Learner Outcomes

By the end of this session, students will be able to
- describe ideas and approaches for problem-solving bullying situations
- identify potential social supports and safe places in a variety of bullying situations

Materials Needed

- Pencils
- Problem-Solving Evaluation Worksheet on page 77
- Sample literature

Preparation Needed

- Each student should have a pencil.
- Gather comic strips, picture books, newspaper or magazine articles, fables, and/or passages from age-appropriate literature that include bullying situations and solutions.
- Make a copy of the worksheet for each student or group.

Class Meeting Outline

Opening Activity (20 minutes)

1. Sometimes it can be difficult to decide how to handle or problem-solve bullying situations.

2. Divide students into groups of three. (See pages 13–14 for ideas and strategies for grouping students.) Give each group one of the bullying samples. Also distribute copies of the worksheet and pencils to each group.

3. **Each group has a sample of a bullying situation. Have one member of your group read the situation. Then have all members discuss the person's or character's solution. Use the questions on the worksheet to evaluate the solution.**

Teacher Tip

You might review each role in the Bullying Circle with the group. A description of the circle can be found on page 24 of the Teacher Guide.

4. Allow the groups time to work. Then have the class come together for discussion. Ask one member of each group to report on its situation and evaluation.

Discussion Questions (25 minutes)

1. **Every situation is slightly different. What factors do you take into account when deciding what is the best approach to help stop bullying?**

2. **What strategies do you rely on to help you solve difficult problems? What kinds of advice or support do you look for? Have you found some things that work better for you?**

3. **What circumstances make it harder or require more courage to step in as a bystander? What are some different options for providing support to the bullied student during and after the bullying situation, and for confronting a student who is bullying before and after the bullying situation?**

4. What role does who you are (in terms of your gender, age, popularity, class) play in how comfortable or effective you are in helping to problem-solve bullying situations and issues?

Wrap-Up

1. There really isn't just one right way to resolve a bullying problem. Sometimes it takes the efforts of more than one person or even several tries before it completely stops. But getting it stopped is important, and efforts must continue until the person is safe and the students who bully stop harming others. Be part of the solution.

2. Encourage additional questions and comments.

Curriculum Connections

Vocabulary: *analyze/critique, nuanced, problem-solving, stereotypes*

Science: Reinforce with students logical steps people use to identify problems, such as developing a hypothesis, testing out theories, and analyzing results. Discuss how problem-solving skills are used in different professions, including politics, business, teaching, and journalism.

Problem-Solving Evaluation Worksheet

Instructions: Use this worksheet to evaluate the solution to bullying in your literature sample.

1. **Types of Bullying:** Identify the type(s) of bullying portrayed.

2. **Stereotypes:** Note whether the piece portrays stereotypes about bullying (such as bullying is always physical or bullying is always done by boys).

3. **Solution:** Rate on a scale of 1–5 whether the solution was (a) effective, (b) safe, and (c) in line with our school rules. ("1" is most effective; "5" is least effective, etc.) For each rating, write one sentence to explain your evaluation.

    a. **Effectiveness Rating:** _____
       Why was or wasn't this an effective solution?

    b. **Safety Rating:** _____
       Why was or wasn't this a safe solution?

    c. **School Rules Rating:** _____
       Why was or wasn't this in line with our school rules?

4. **Other Solutions:** Write one or two other solutions and pros and cons for each.

Category 4

Hot Spots

(Five class meetings)

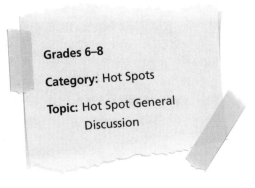

Grades 6–8

Category: Hot Spots

Topic: Hot Spot General Discussion

Hot Spots Are Here!

Background

No one knows better than students which areas in and around school are likely to be "hot spots" for bullying. Start your discussion about hot spots by listening to students' experiences and opinions. Allow this meeting to be student-directed as much as possible. This class meeting should precede the four specific "hot spot" class meetings (found on pages 83–102).

Learner Outcomes

By the end of this session, students will be able to

- identify places in and around school where bullying is most likely to occur
- describe ways that student behaviors vary according to different circumstances or places and reasons for those differences
- describe ways that student behavior contributes to bullying
- share ideas about ways adults could improve supervision and respond in hot spots

Materials Needed

- Paper and pencils
- Tape
- Chalkboard and chalk or dry erase board and markers

- Two sheets of chart paper to cover OBQ data
- Data from the OBQ regarding the hot spots in your school (question 18)

Preparation Needed

- Read through the data from the OBQ (question 18, on page 65 of the survey report). On a chalkboard or dry erase board, make a chart with three columns: Hot Spot, Percentage Bullied Here, and Ranking. Under the first heading, list all hot spots for bullying in random order. Under the second heading, write the percentage of students who reported being bullied in each location. Under the third heading, indicate the ranking of each hot spot (where 1 indicates the hot spot where most bullying takes place).
- Cover the first column with one sheet of paper, and the last two columns with another sheet of paper.

Class Meeting Outline

Opening Activity (10 minutes)

1. **Who remembers the question on the Olweus Bullying Questionnaire that asked where you have been bullied? We call these places "hot spots." Today we're going to discuss where students said hot spots were located in our school, and talk about ways we can make them safer.**

2. Split the class into two teams. (See pages 13–14 for ideas and strategies for dividing your class into groups or teams.)

3. Provide a sheet of paper and a pencil to each team. Ask teams to appoint one person to record answers on the paper and signal when the team has completed the task.

4. Instruct each team to prepare its paper by writing Hot Spot Rankings at the top of the page; then write the numbers 1 through 5 down the left side of the page. Explain that they will use the data from the questionnaire to rank the top five hot spots (with 1 being the worst/most common hot spot) in their school.

5. Uncover the first column on the board (leave percentages and rankings covered) and instruct each team to begin. Have the teams signal that they have finished.

6. Invite the team that signaled first to share its findings in rank order. Then have the second team read its results (citing differences, if any). Reveal the percentages and rankings from the OBQ on the board and discuss differences.

Teacher Tip

In each class meeting, always assume that there are students present who have bullied others, as well as students who have been bullied. The majority of students in your class are likely to be bystanders who are questioning what to do when they see bullying behavior in their peers. Ask students not to name names or use too many details in describing bullying that is happening in your school's hot spots.

Discussion Questions (20 minutes)

1. **Were any of you surprised at which locations turned out to be hot spots? Why?**

2. **Were any of you surprised about the rankings? Why or why not?**

3. **Why do you think these five locations are hot spots in our school? What factors play a part in making them hot spots?**

4. **In what ways do you think students behave differently in hot spots than in other parts of the school? Why?**

5. **What factors might make one place feel like a hot spot for some people, and not for others?**

6. **Were there differences between how boys and girls identified hot spots?**

7. Have students do the following with a partner. **List areas in our school that you would identify as "safe spots." Do you and your partner agree? Discuss why or why not.**

8. **What are some things that adults in our school could do to make hot spots safer?**

9. **What are some things that students could do to make hot spots feel safer?** List the students' action ideas on chart paper.

Teacher Tips

• Be sure to follow through on student and adult action plans. Report back to your class the steps adults are taking to address bullying and improve safety and supervision in hot spots. Assess the impact student action plans are having. Make improvements as needed.

• Refer to pages 40–42 in the Teacher Guide for ideas about improving supervision in hot spots.

Wrap-Up

1. **Figuring out places where bullying happens is an important part of bullying prevention. It also helps us to understand more about it. Today we discussed some ideas about ways we can work together to turn hot**

spots into safe spots. Let's try these ideas out for two weeks and then come back together to talk about how our solutions are making a difference. We might need to adjust our actions to improve things further.

2. Encourage additional questions and comments.

Curriculum Connections

Vocabulary: *comparison, hot spots, rank order, statistics*

English:

- Have students write about ways to make a particular hot spot feel safer for all students.

- Instruct students to write an action plan for themselves with the following four questions: What can I do to make sure I don't contribute to bullying behavior? What can my friends and I do to help others in hot spots? Which adults at school and at home would I personally turn to in cases of bullying at our school? What assistance would I like to receive from adults?

Math: Have students use OBQ data to create bar or pie-chart graphs showing differences in hot spots for girls compared to hot spots for boys. Discuss reasons for differences and similarities.

Social Studies:

- Point out how the term *hot spots* does not always refer to places in school buildings. Let students know that it is often used to talk about world problems. Have students refer to current events to find out what areas of the world are identified as hot spots and why.

- Divide students into groups to consider hot spots based on politics/war, environmental issues, famine or other natural disasters, diseases such as AIDS, human rights, or children's rights. Suggest that they use the Internet to research organizations that deal with hot spots such as Amnesty International, International Red Cross, World Health Organization, Green Peace, and Human Rights Networks. Instruct each group to highlight hot spots for its category and list at least three factors that make a location a hot spot.

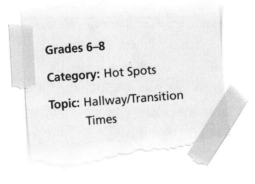

Grades 6–8

Category: Hot Spots

Topic: Hallway/Transition
Times

Hallway Hazards

Background

Transition times at school can provide enjoyable breaks and opportunities to socialize with peers, but they can also be prime times when bullying occurs because adult presence is less concentrated. Although it is the primary responsibility of adults to provide careful supervision in hallways and during transition times, it is also helpful to talk about strategies students can use to stay safe and to help each other as well. This class meeting may require two sessions.

Learner Outcomes

By the end of this session, students will be able to
- identify the hallway areas where bullying is most likely to occur
- give reasons why students' behavior may vary in different circumstances and places
- describe ways adult and peer support can make transition times feel safer
- identify practical bystander strategies to deal with other students who are exhibiting bullying behaviors during transition times

Materials Needed

- Role-Play Scenarios on page 87
- Tape or chalk
- Role-Play Evaluation Worksheet on pages 88–89

Preparation Needed

- Select and copy four scenarios to use for class role-play, or write scenarios that focus on real problems experienced in your school.
- In your classroom space, use tape or chalk lines to represent a "hallway" (include lockers, stairwells, and doors). Alternatively, conduct this activity in the hallway when it is not being used.
- Make four copies of the Role-Play Evaluation Worksheet, one for each small group.

Class Meeting Outline

Opening Activity (15 minutes)

1. **Passing between classes can be a time to socialize with friends, but it's also a time when lots of students complain about being bullied. Hallways were the number X hot spot identified on our school questionnaire.** (Refer to rankings identified in prior class meeting.)
2. **In today's class meeting, we're going to use scenarios to role-play possible solutions to bullying problems in hallways.**
3. Divide the class into four groups for the role-play activity. (See pages 13–14 for ideas and strategies for dividing your class into groups.) Give each group one of the four scenarios you have chosen for role-play.
4. To prepare for the role-play, ask each group to
   - practice role-playing one way of handling the scenario using positive, assertive action on the part of bystanders
   - act out only their positive solution—not the bullying incident
   - focus on actions student bystanders can take instead of getting an adult involved
5. Provide an opportunity for each group to act out its solution for the class. Describe the scenario for the class prior to the group's role-play.
6. After each role-play, ask students to work in their groups to critique the solutions, using the Role-Play Evaluation Worksheet. As a large group, briefly brainstorm other positive alternatives. If students role-play actions that are not positive, talk about why and discuss potential consequences for those choices.

7. Ask students to comment on their experience of playing their role. Focus on the sense of power they felt helping, how it felt working as a group of bystanders as opposed to by oneself, etc.

Discussion Questions (15 minutes)

1. **Why do some students use the hallway/transition times as opportunities to bully others?**

2. **Why do you think bullying continues to be a problem in the hall? Are there particular hallways or areas in the hall that present more difficulties? What else can be done to reduce bullying in those spots?**

3. **When students are bullied repeatedly in places like our school's hallways, how do you think it affects their feelings about school in general?**

4. **What would you like adults to do when they learn about bullying in a hallway?**

5. **Do you think the hallway experience is different for boys and girls? How so?** Ask students to consider this same question for students in a social or ethnic minority, for those with disabilities, for younger students, for those who aren't considered popular, or for new students.

Dig Deeper

Utilize student-written scenarios for other role-play and discussion opportunities that are less teacher-directed.

Teacher Tips

- Check in with your students regularly to see if ideas they generated have been useful, or if they still need assistance to work on hallway bullying problems.

- Talk about the intervention steps school staff will use when they see bullying happening. These steps are outlined on pages 87–91 of the Teacher Guide.

- Extend this activity/discussion over an additional class meeting time to allow all groups to act out their scenarios.

Wrap-Up

1. **The adults at our school know that hallways are hot spots for bullying and we are taking steps to make our hallways safer by** (describe/give examples). **You can help as well. If you see someone being bullied in our hallways, tell an adult. Don't assume others will! We will work to make it stop. We also expect that you will work together and use positive solutions to help classmates like those we've talked about here. If you have bullied others in the hallway, remember there are disciplinary consequences for those actions, so consider making better decisions about how you choose to behave.**

2. Encourage additional questions and comments.

Curriculum Connections

Vocabulary: *assertive, assist, peer, social minority, transition times*

English:

- Ask students to write about the challenges of being a bystander who encounters a bullying situation on the way to class. Have them focus on how it would feel. What factors would determine how much courage it would take to get involved? What factors might keep them from intervening/helping? What supports would they need to feel safe enough to assist?

- Have students think about a time they bullied another student (or watched and didn't get involved). Suggest they write a letter to that student telling how they felt and what they would do differently if they could go back in time.

Community Service: Encourage students to create an anti-bullying newsletter with tips for avoiding or minimizing bullying in hot spots like the hallway.

Social Studies: Have students research people who showed courage to "do the right thing" in the face of difficult odds. Suggest areas such as civil and human rights, sports, and medicine.

Role-Play Scenarios

Instructions: Copy the cards and cut them apart. Give each group one role-play scenario.

Every day between classes, Ben makes it a point to slam into John hard enough to knock him into the lockers and send John's books flying. "Oh, Dude!" his tormentor smirks and sarcastically says, "I'm so sorry!"

Jen often stops to get her books for the next class at her locker. As students pass, they've made a game out of either saying mean things to her, or taking something out of her locker and playing Keep-away.

Each day a group of students follow Dillon very closely. All the time they are right behind him, they are calling him mean names—whispering softly enough that supervising adults don't notice. They also threaten that they will "take care of him" after school.

The "cool girls" all stick together in the hallway. Between classes, they laugh at other girls, mock their choice of clothes and their choice of friends. They also spread rumors about the other girls.

Mosliah immigrated with his family from Iraq just a year ago. Many of the boys in the class call him "Osama" and "Terrorist". They often stick nasty notes to his locker.

Role-Play Evaluation Worksheet

Scenario 1

Was it safe?

Was it effective? (Did it stop the bullying behavior?)

Was it realistic?

Did the bystanders work together?

Were there missed opportunities to assist?

Comments

Scenario 2

Was it safe?

Was it effective? (Did it stop the bullying behavior?)

Was it realistic?

Did the bystanders work together?

Were there missed opportunities to assist?

Comments

Role-Play Evaluation Worksheet (continued)

Scenario 3

Was it safe?

Was it effective? (Did it stop the bullying behavior?)

Was it realistic?

Did the bystanders work together?

Were there missed opportunities to assist?

Comments

Scenario 4

Was it safe?

Was it effective? (Did it stop the bullying behavior?)

Was it realistic?

Did the bystanders work together?

Were there missed opportunities to assist?

Comments

Grades 6–8

Category: Hot Spots

Topic: Bullying in Physical Education Classes, Bathrooms, and Locker Rooms

Not Just Locker Room Talk

Background

Physical changes during adolescence can lead to student anxiety and concerns about body image, physical coordination, self-esteem, and sexuality. Physical education classes, locker rooms, and bathrooms can be places where students are particularly vulnerable to unwanted comments or bullying about their bodies and the physical changes they are undergoing. These comments and behaviors are often related to differences in rates of physical development and how students compare to ideal images of masculinity or femininity. Common insults, such as being called "gay" or other sexual innuendos or put-downs must be considered serious and be addressed consistently and swiftly by adults. Research shows potential links between this type of bullying and hazing and sexual harassment. It is also important to be aware that this type of bullying may occur outside of school at sporting events, community swimming pools, scouting events, and the like, but the impact is often carried over to student relationships with peers at school.

Learner Outcomes

By the end of this session, students will be able to
- identify examples of bullying in locker rooms, PE classes, and bathrooms
- discuss why the types of bullying that occur in these locations may feel particularly devastating to those being bullied
- describe strategies to address bullying behavior in these environments

Materials Needed

- Paper
- Pencils
- Index cards
- Container for each team

Preparation Needed

- Refer to your school policy and procedures on bullying and/or cyber bullying, if one exists.
- Identify six to eight bullying scenarios to read to the class (number each). Include examples such as:
  - Students roll their eyes or "make way" in an exaggerated manner when overweight students come near them in PE class.
  - Students make fun of a girl in the locker room who undresses under her towel.
  - You hear someone being called gay.
  - You notice that one student is always picked last for teams because he or she is considered uncoordinated.
  - You see a boy snapping a girl's bra during PE class, while others look on and laugh.
  - Someone laughs and makes fun of another classmate as that person is showering.
  - Two bigger students snap their towels at several smaller students in the locker room.
  - Someone took another student's underwear and hid it in a vacant locker.
  - Several students make fun of how another student throws a ball during PE.
  - In the bathroom, you witness two students making very nasty comments to another student about his or her acne.
- Number a set of index cards for each team according to the number of scenarios you will use (e.g., 1–6).

Class Meeting Outline

Opening Activity (15 minutes)

Teacher Tips

- Issues around real or perceived differences in sexual orientation may arise in this meeting. Remind students that sexual put-downs and language are never acceptable. Refer to the fact sheet entitled "Bullying Among Children and Youth on Perceptions and Differences in Sexual Orientation" from www.stopbullyingnow.hrsa.gov.

- Each teacher in the school system should have a copy of Title IX rights. You can find information on Title IX at www.usdoj.gov/crt/cor/coord/ixlegal.php or www.titleix.info.

1. **We know that students may be subjected to some very personal kinds of bullying (or worse) in places like the locker rooms, the bathrooms, and PE class.**

    As a way to discuss these issues, we're going to do an exercise, during which you'll have to work as a team to find solutions for bullying situations. Once I read a situation, each team will have one minute to discuss the situation and write down a positive way of resolving it on the index card for that scenario. The cards I'll give you are numbered, so be sure to write on the correct card. We'll all then decide which are the best solutions. Remind students that the ideas must be respectful and suggest a positive, real-life solution.

2. Divide students into four teams. (See pages 13–14 for ideas and strategies for grouping students.) Hand out a pencil and numbered index cards to each team. Give each team a container.

3. Read aloud the first situation. After getting ideas from their teammates, one player writes the group's solution on index card 1 and then drops it into the team's container. Continue reading each scenario in sequence.

4. Once all the scenarios have been read, collect the solution cards for each team. Briefly review each scenario and read each group's suggested solution.

Discussion Questions (15 minutes)

1. **What are the pros and cons of each solution? How realistic is the solution? how safe? How likely is it to end positively?** Ask students to raise their hands to vote on the best solution for each scenario. Note that students may not vote for their own solution.

2. **What was it like to have to come up with positive responses "on the spot"?**

3. It's hard for adults to think on the spot as well. What are some reasons that make it difficult for you in real-life situations?

4. Sometimes bullying in the bathrooms or locker rooms can be cyber bullying. How can cyber bullying occur in these places? (One possible response may be taking pictures or videos of vulnerable classmates with the intent to put these online.) **What should be done about these situations?** (Review your school policy regarding cyber bullying, especially in this manner, and discuss ways to report these incidents.)

5. What can we do if we see or experience bullying in the locker room? What can adults do to prevent locker room bullying? What can you as students do to stop locker room bullying?

Teacher Tip

Students may not be aware of the difference between bullying, hazing, and sexual harassment. Provide accurate definitions and consequences of each. Hazing and sexual harassment pose significant safety and liability issues for schools, particularly if these behaviors are minimized by mislabeling them as bullying. Know your responsibilities in supervising and protecting student rights.

Wrap-Up

1. There are times when we all feel awkward or uncomfortable about our bodies and how we look. It's never right to tease someone that way, especially at times or in places where we feel vulnerable or privacy is limited.

   I hope that our discussion today has helped you to think about ways you can alter your own conduct and to stand up for peers who are being bullied or harassed in places like the locker room or bathrooms. If you feel uncomfortable or threatened in these situations, it's especially important to tell an adult you trust.

2. Encourage additional questions and comments.

Curriculum Connections

Vocabulary: *growth spurt, hazing, resolution, sexual harassment, vulnerable*

English:

- Have students write about a time when they went through a particularly awkward phase of growth. How did they feel? How did they handle it?

- Have students write an advice column for young teens offering a positive way to handle a problem such as growth spurts, weight fluctuations, awkward phases, bad hair days, acne, an embarrassing moment, being chosen last for a team, or dealing with sexual or humiliating put-downs about appearance.

Physical Education/Health:

- Encourage students to learn about normal growth during adolescence. Discuss respecting differences and role-play ways of setting appropriate boundaries.

- Discuss how gender-role stereotyping in sports contributes to bullying (for example, boys who are not good at or don't like sports, girls or boys who get involved in sports traditionally played by the opposite sex).

- Research ways that media set (or influence) standards about what it means to be a "normal" teen boy or girl (body image, activities, dress, etc.).

Social Studies:

- Research and discuss with students Title IX rights of students involved in extracurricular sports.

- Discuss legal issues (hazing, harassment, sexual discrimination, racial or gender discrimination) related to participation in sports. Present students with actual cases or selected vignettes to identify when behaviors have crossed the line from bullying to hazing or sexual harassment.

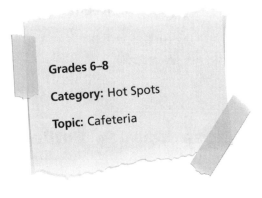

Grades 6–8

Category: Hot Spots

Topic: Cafeteria

Cafeteria Challenges

Background

What more challenging place is there to deal with being bullied than the school cafeteria? In dinner-theater fashion, the cafeteria is a stage where the social dynamics of peer relations are played out. It is here, in the cafeteria, that cliques may be the most visible. Social groups may sit together, often at the same table each day. In this environment, it's very evident which students sit alone and may not have a social group. The cafeteria is a perfect setting for bullying to occur. But the cafeteria is also an ideal place for bystanders to stand up to bullying behavior.

Learner Outcomes

By the end of this session, students will be able to
- identify the types of bullying that occur in their school's cafeteria
- identify the motivations and social dynamics that come into play
- describe strategies to prevent and deal with bullying in the cafeteria

Materials Needed

- Tape

Preparation Needed

- Clear an area in your classroom space (such as a wide aisle) large enough for the class to form a circle.

Class Meeting Outline

Opening Activity (10 minutes)

1. Ask all students to stand in a circle in the open space that you've created in your classroom.
2. Place a strip of tape down the middle of the circle.
3. **I will read some statements and I want you to move to this side** (indicate) **if you agree, or this side** (indicate) **if you disagree. If you aren't sure or have no preference, stand on the tape line in the middle. There is no right answer, and it may be difficult for you to decide, so go with your first reaction . . . and be honest.**
4. Use the following statements or create some of your own:

   - I would rather have a group of friends than one best friend.
   - I would rather feel embarrassed than afraid.
   - I feel pressure to hang out with certain people all the time instead of feeling free to make new friends.
   - I would rather sit alone in the cafeteria than to have an assigned seat with people I don't know.
   - I would like to have a regular group to sit with at lunch even if they don't like me (or pay attention to me or include me in the conversation) rather than sit by myself.
   - If I see someone sitting alone, I try to distance myself from that person rather than try to get to know him or her.
   - If I had a friend who was being bullied by a group of students, I would step in to defend him or her rather than ignore it.

Dig Deeper

- Find a time to talk with students who appear to be repeatedly isolated or bullied at lunchtime. Strategize ways to make your school's cafeteria experience more welcoming and less distressing for them. Discuss an action plan to help them feel safe.

- For those students who have particular difficulty with social skills, and who might be at additional risk for being bullied, arrange a separate time to practice modeling social skills in small-group settings.

- If I saw a new student or someone I didn't know well struggling to find a place to sit in the cafeteria, I'd invite that person to join me.

Discussion Questions (20 minutes)

1. What are some things you noticed about people's responses in this activity?
2. Was it hard to be honest about your feelings? Why or why not?
3. In general, how would you describe lunchtime at our school? How many of you would describe it as pleasant? unpleasant? What factors does it depend on (for example, you are having a bad day, you are not popular, your best friend is not in school)?
4. If someone was attending our school for the first time today and he or she asked you to explain who sits where in our school cafeteria and why, what would you say? Where would you suggest a new student sit and what kinds of things would you think about when giving him or her this advice?
5. If you had to eat alone in our school cafeteria, what would that experience be like? When you are tense or afraid, where in your body do you feel it? What's it like to eat when you are feeling anxious, nervous, or afraid?
6. What might be challenging about inviting someone you usually don't sit with to join you at your table?
7. Do students have a responsibility to include others who are left out?
8. What might you do if you were looking for a group to join at lunch? How might you try making a connection with someone?
9. If you had a friend who was being excluded or made fun of in the cafeteria, what would you do?
10. People who bully tend to do so in front of an audience. Why do you think that is?
11. What can you do when you see bullying happening in our school cafeteria? What can you do if you are being bullied in our school cafeteria?

Dig Deeper

- Take an occasional walk through your school's cafeteria to observe your students' behavior and notice how they are grouped together. Be sure to intervene if you see bullying behavior.

- Be sure to share observations about lunchtime bullying with other adults at school who have regular contact with the students involved. It is important for staff to intervene consistently.

Wrap-Up

1. **Although lunch is a time when you should have a chance to relax and hang out with your friends, the cafeteria can be difficult for many students. It is a place where we know bullying occurs.**

   But it's also a great opportunity to show courage and to be an active and helpful bystander. Try to work together to include students who are being isolated or bullied by using some of the strategies we have talked about today.

2. Encourage additional questions and comments.

Curriculum Connections

Vocabulary: *isolated, manners, polite, social dynamics, social skills*

Social Studies/Health/Community Service: Introduce the idea of a Mix It Up at Lunch Day in the cafeteria and involve students in planning the event. For more information, see www.tolerance.org/teens/.

English/Art: Suggest that students write skits or vignettes or draw cartoons showing positive ways to deal with bullying in the cafeteria. They can use the statements read during the opening activity or the discussion questions for ideas.

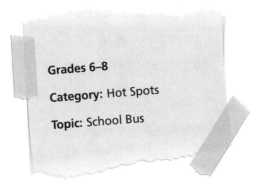

Grades 6–8

Category: Hot Spots

Topic: School Bus

The Secret Life of the School Bus

Background

The bus environment, like the cafeteria, is a snapshot of both positive and negative aspects of peer relationships. When mixed-age groups of students ride the same bus, younger or more vulnerable students tend to become the focus of teasing and bullying. Because bus drivers are often the only adult on the bus and must obviously focus their attention on safe driving, many bus-related bullying incidents aren't addressed promptly or even addressed at all. Bus drivers often describe feeling helpless, frustrated, and disrespected. In schools where students car-pool or walk home rather than take a bus, some of the same issues may still occur.

Learner Outcomes

By the end of this session, students will be able to
- identify the challenges of the school bus experience
- describe how social groups at school carry over into transportation situations
- explain why the bus can be an environment that lends itself to bullying behavior
- describe ways to address bullying behavior on the school bus, in car pools, and while walking to and from school

Materials Needed

- Large sheets of chart paper (one per group of two to four students)
- Black markers (one per group of two to four students)
- Masking tape
- Paper and pencils
- Examples of storyboards (graphic novels, comic strips, etc.)

Preparation Needed

- Look for storyboards on the Internet and print several examples. One good site is www.storyboards-east.com/storybrd.htm.
- Gather a sufficient number of supplies for your class size.
- Provide space on tables or the floor for writing and drawing on the sheets of paper.
- The concept of "storyboarding" could be introduced in another class (English or Art) before this class meeting to save time during the class meeting.

Class Meeting Outline

Opening Activity (20 minutes)

1. **How many of you have seen incidents of bullying on the school bus, whether traveling to and from school or on a field trip? Or, if you walk or car-pool to school, have you seen any bullying incidents during that time? Without naming names, what happened? Did anyone defend the student who was being bullied?**

2. **Today we're going to discuss appropriate actions you can take when you're in these situations.**

3. Divide the class into groups of two to four students. (See pages 13–14 for ideas and strategies for grouping students.)

4. Equip each small group with a large sheet of paper and a black marker, paper, and a pencil.

5. Ask students if they are familiar with storyboards. (Storyboards are a panel or a series of panels that show in sequence the important changes in a scene or story. Writers and illustrators use storyboards

to create ad campaigns, commercials, cartoons, and TV shows.) Show examples of storyboards to the class.

6. Instruct each small group to create a short storyboard (four to six panels) that depicts a bullying incident on a school bus, followed by a positive, safe solution to stop the bullying and/or actively assist the bullied student(s). Encourage creativity! Students may wish to sketch a sample in pencil on scratch paper before drawing on the chart paper.

7. Invite a representative from each group to show its storyboard to the class and describe the solution. Allow the other groups to give feedback.

Dig Deeper

Resources such as the *Peaceful School Bus Program* show how building a sense of community among riders on a bus helps to prevent bullying. For more information, refer to www.hazelden .org/web/go/peacefulschoolbus.

Discussion Questions (10 minutes)

1. **What kinds of things did you consider in designing your storyboards? in crafting a solution?**

2. **How do you get to and from school each day? How long does it take you to get to and from school each day? What do you like and dislike about the "journey"? How does this routine affect your mood or experience each day?**

3. **Are there assigned seats on the bus? If not, do students sit in the same or in different places each day? What roles do age, gender, and popularity play in determining where students sit? How does that carry over into cliques or groups at school? Do the same people sit with each other on the bus as at school?**

4. **Why do you think problems crop up on the bus or in car pools? How does the bus environment lend itself to bullying behavior?**

5. **What do you like and dislike about riding the bus for field trips? How does this experience affect the field trip and the rest of your day?**

6. **What are some things that you can do if you see bullying behavior while on the bus, walking, or car-pooling? What are some things that you can do to prevent bullying behavior in these locations?**

7. **Do the school rules against bullying apply to student behavior on the bus? Why?**

Dig Deeper

• Younger students may feel safer on a bus if they know an older student is looking out for them. Cross-grade collaborative activities (such as "reading buddies") can help build relationships between younger students and older students.

• Ask your school's Bullying Prevention Coordinating Committee to post the four anti-bullying rules in student buses. This will help to reinforce the idea that the rules are to be followed on the bus as well as on the school grounds.

Wrap-Up

1. Review the key points discussed in this class meeting. Invite students to share one idea that they can put into practice when on the bus, in a car pool, or walking to and from school.

2. Post the storyboards in the classroom.

Curriculum Connections

Vocabulary: *storyboard, transportation*

Art: Encourage students to put their storyboards into motion—creating an animated cartoon, role-play or skit, or video.

Social Studies:

- Have students discuss laws/rules that apply to school bus behavior. Invite the school transportation director (or a bus driver) to speak about bus drivers' experiences, their training, and regulations for transporting students. Invite students to brainstorm ways to make the school bus a safer environment. Discuss the following questions: How can you stand up for those who are targeted? What can adults do to help? What can bus drivers or parents driving car pools do?

- Highlight the Rosa Parks bus story and the Montgomery Bus Boycott of 1955–1956. Relate how the bus at that time was a snapshot of the civil rights struggle. Discuss the role power played in this situation. Be sure to emphasize that this is not an example of bullying, but of racial discrimination.

Category **5**

....

Peer Relationships

(Ten class meetings)

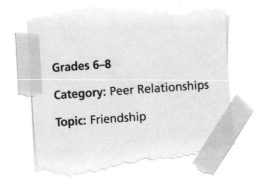

Grades 6–8

Category: Peer Relationships

Topic: Friendship

Friends—Who Needs Them?

Background

Close relationships with peers are an important element of health and well-being at every stage of life. Friendships play an even more key role during adolescence. During adolescence, students begin to reinvent themselves and to make friends with others they see as having similar interests and values. Students need help differentiating between true friends and more superficial relationships, and they need adult guidance in productive social interactions. While most students this age have several friends, be especially aware of students who have no close friends. These students are more likely to feel socially isolated and are at higher risk for being bullied by their classmates.

Learner Outcomes

By the end of this session, students will be able to

- list four reasons why it is important to have at least one friend
- list qualities to look for in a friend
- describe how to show respect to others who are not in their friendship circle
- describe how friendship circles will change as they change

Materials Needed

- Pencils

- Chalkboard and chalk or dry erase board and markers
- Job Description for a Close Friend on page 108

Preparation Needed

- Make sure each student has a pencil.
- Make one copy of the handout for each student.

Class Meeting Outline

Opening Activity (10 minutes)

1. On the board write "acquaintance," "friend," and "best friend." **What is the difference between an acquaintance and a friend? What is the difference between a friend and a best friend? Do you behave the same way with best friends as with acquaintances? Why or why not?**

2. **Those people we call our best friends may better be described as our closest friends. I want you to think about traits or qualities you look for in a good friend and to write a job description for an ideal close friend.** Give a handout to each student and briefly review what each element of the job description means. Allow students to work individually for a few minutes.

3. **The traits and qualities you expect in good friends should also be traits and qualities you expect in yourself. On your job description, put a check mark beside those traits you believe you possess and circle those that may need work.**

4. Have students refer to their job descriptions to process this activity.

Dig Deeper

Look for ways to help friendless students have positive experiences and personal interactions in class. This may help them to cultivate friendships and social support networks outside of class.

Discussion Questions (20 minutes)

1. **What things do you look for in a close friend? Is it hard to find someone who meets all these qualifications? Have your ideas or expectations changed over time?**

2. **What are the most important things about having at least one friend? What is most important about having a friend here at school?**

3. **What are some possible challenges of finding a really close friend?**

4. **What are some of the challenges of *being* a good friend?**

5. **What are the risks of choosing the wrong friend? What might make a person the wrong friend for you?** (Answers might include he or she may not be available when you need a friend, doesn't keep confidences, may use you to get what he or she wants, isn't always nice to you, or is involved in risky activities.)

6. **For students your age, how can friends be a positive influence on behavior?**

7. **In your opinion, how can peer pressure from friends have a negative influence on the behavior of students your age?**

8. **What are some examples of ways you can be a positive influence on your friends? How can you influence them positively when it comes to the issue of bullying?**

9. **Are friendships different for boys and for girls? How does gender affect ways you interact with each other?**

10. **Over time, friendships can change. This is a normal part of growing up, and it even happens with adults. But when it happens, it can really hurt! How can you be considerate of a former friend?** (Answers might include keeping the secrets that you know about that person, never using information to bully or gossip about that person, keeping old confidences private, being polite/saying hi when you pass the person in the hall, or not "dissing" the person.)

11. **If you know of people (no names) who are isolated or who have no close friends, what are some good ways to include them or look out for them?**

12. **It is unrealistic for us to think that everyone at school has to be friends with everyone else! But we all need to be able to coexist and find ways to be respectful and accepting of each other. How can you treat other students kindly even if you don't consider them to be a friend? even if you don't like them?**

Teacher Tips

- As with other sessions, allow discussions to evolve without rushing students. Extend the topic to additional class meetings if desired by you and the class.

- Suggest that parents and guardians read the U.S. Department of Education's article "Friendship—Helping Your Child Through Early Adolescence" at www.ed.gov/parents/academic/help/adolescence/part9.html. (It's a good idea for you to read this too!)

Wrap-Up

1. **Friendships help us during life's ups and downs. Friends are people to share and do things with. Friends provide emotional support when we need it. We need friends in order to stay happy and healthy.**

   But there are times when all of us (adults too) feel let down or hurt by our friends. So our challenge this week is to think about how we can be a better friend to others and try to include people who might be feeling left out.

2. Encourage additional questions and comments.

Curriculum Connections

Vocabulary: *acquaintance, benefits or perks, coexist, duties, good friendships, job description, qualifications, responsibilities*

Science: Ask students to create hypotheses about either the positive or negative effects of friendships on peers their age. Then have them conduct interviews to test and evaluate their hypotheses.

English: Use age-appropriate literature to illustrate how good and/or bad friendships can affect young people (*Stargirl* or other stories by Jerry Spinelli, *Tangerine* by Edward Bloor, *The Opposite of Fate* by Amy Tan).

Job Description for a Close Friend

1. **Duties, Responsibilities, or Tasks**
   (What kinds of things do you expect a close friend to do in order to demonstrate his or her friendship?)

2. **Qualifications Needed**
   (What interests, qualities, or traits are you looking for in a close friend?)

3. **Experience Needed**
   (Do you expect this person to be a proven good friend to others?)

4. **Hours Available**
   (Do you expect this person to be available whenever you need him/her? Or only when it is convenient for him/her?)

5. **Benefits of the Position**
   (What can this person expect from you in return?)

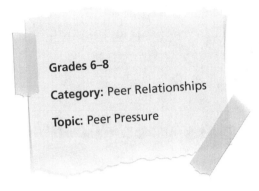

Grades 6–8

Category: Peer Relationships

Topic: Peer Pressure

Positive and Negative Peer Pressure

Background

The need to fit in can lead students to be greatly influenced by peer pressure. Peer pressure can cause students to do things they wouldn't normally do, such as skip class, participate in bullying, and become involved in risky behaviors. It's important for students to learn skills to resist negative peer pressure and to stand firm on personal boundaries. Although peer pressure is mostly associated with harmful influences, it can have positive influences as well. Positive peer pressure provides group support to resist negative influences. It can encourage students to work toward goals like getting better grades, participating in positive extracurricular activities, and standing up for others.

Learner Outcomes

By the end of this session, students will be able to

- list examples of the types of peer pressure they feel
- describe positive and negative aspects of peer pressure
- identify ways to counter negative peer pressure

Materials Needed

- Paper and pencils
- Chalkboard and chalk or dry erase board and markers

Preparation Needed

- Make sure each student has paper and a pencil.
- Review the sample vocabulary words.

Class Meeting Outline

Opening Activity (10 minutes)

1. **We all want to fit in, to feel like we belong at school and elsewhere. And sometimes we make choices that don't feel right or match the way we usually think or act, just to be part of the crowd.**

2. Review what peer pressure is and ask students to give general examples (no names). **Why do you think peer pressure exists? Does it have a purpose?**

3. Give each student a blank sheet of paper and pencil. Instruct students to quickly sketch a figure of themselves (stick figures are good enough). Draw a large stick figure on the board as students are drawing their figures.

4. Next ask the students to reflect on different types of peer pressure they have experienced and write or illustrate them around the figure.

5. **Look at the examples of peer pressure you have included on your paper. Find the top five in terms of how strongly they influence or affect you. Rank them from 1 to 5, with 1 indicating the most influence.**

6. Gather students in a circle to process and debrief the activity.

Teacher Tip

Be clear to students that peer pressure, however powerful, never negates individual responsibility.

Discussion Questions (20 minutes)

1. **What different forms of peer pressure have you experienced?** Write students' responses on the board.

   a. Draw a dotted line through the center of the large stick figure on the board. Invite the class to share different forms of peer pressures they have experienced. Write them around the figure, placing boys' responses by the left half of the figure and girls' responses on the right half.

   b. Encourage students to discuss impressions, ideas, and
      "aha" moments.

2. **Do you think peer pressures are the same for boys and girls? If not, how are they different?**

3. **Do you think students in elementary school and students in middle school experience different kinds of peer pressure? If so, in what ways?**

4. **Is the peer pressure students your age experience different from pressures your parents experienced when they were your age? If so, how?**

5. Have students pair up and ask their partner: **If you could get rid of one type of peer pressure, what would it be and why?**

6. **What's one thing you'd change in our class or school to reduce the pressure kids feel to go along with the crowd?**

7. **In your opinion, what is more important: fitting in or doing the right thing? What factors might affect your feelings about this?** (Students might say the specific situation, whom you are with, where you are, whether you are popular or not.)

8. **Sometimes it's hard to know what to say when you are feeling pressured by peers to do something you know is wrong or that feels wrong for you. It's easy to feel flustered or embarrassed when you are put on the spot. None of us want to be labeled "uncool" or a "goody-goody."** Invite students to brainstorm responses kids their age can make that wouldn't make them sound uncool.

9. **Why do you think people go along with things they know aren't right? What does it feel like physically to go along with something you know to be wrong? What does it feel like emotionally?**

10. **Peer pressure isn't always bad. Can anyone tell about a time when peer pressure led you to make a better choice or to do something positive? How are decisions to go along with positive peer pressure different from decisions to go along with negative peer pressure?**

Wrap-Up

1. **It is a very human desire to want to fit in, and peer pressure can be a difficult aspect of life to deal with. Sometimes it's hard to know when and if to give in to it, and when and if to stand firm against it.**

   We all need to make decisions to rise above the crowd and do what's right, even when it's not popular to do so. This week's challenge is to try to notice the different ways peer pressure affects your life and your school's social environment, in both good and bad ways.

2. Encourage additional questions and comments.

Curriculum Connections

Vocabulary: *peer pressure, positive peer pressure, negative peer pressure*

English:

- Have students write about a time they felt pulled by peer pressure to do something they didn't want to do. Ask them to describe ways they resisted and whether or not they were effective.

- Have students interview parents about peer pressures they felt when they were in middle school.

- Encourage students to write about a time they chose to stand up as an individual against negative peer pressure.

Social Studies/History/Civics: Ask students to research and write about social activists or humanitarians who chose to go against popular views in order to work for positive social changes or to right an injustice.

Health/Physical Education: Have students list high-risk activities that their peers might feel pressure to engage in (alcohol or other drug use, smoking, breaking rules at home or school, etc.). Have them role-play specific words and actions they could use to resist (but not lose face).

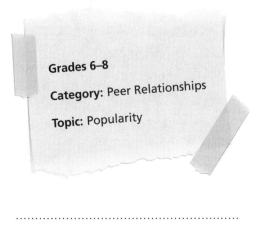

Grades 6–8

Category: Peer Relationships

Topic: Popularity

Look Beyond the Label

Background

Being popular can be a fluid, somewhat arbitrary designation, yet most students in a school would be able to identify students who are considered popular. There is nothing inherently wrong with being popular, but popularity at this age is often based on superficial qualities. Many students may feel conflicted about which peers to befriend or spend time with based on their social status. In this class meeting, you will encourage students to consider factors that determine whether someone is viewed as popular or unpopular in school. Challenge them to consider positive responsibilities of being popular, such as being a positive influence on others, rather than exerting power over others in a negative way.

Learner Outcomes

By the end of this session, students will be able to
- identify characteristics that make someone popular in their school
- identify ways that popularity can be used either as a positive influence or as a negative influence
- list and define social labels that may exist for groups in their school
- discuss how these labels can impact individual students
- understand that although some students who bully are popular, striving for their friendship can have negative results

Materials Needed

- Colored adhesive dots or small circles cut from slips of colored construction paper (equal numbers of 3 different colors, enough that each student in your class would get one)
- Tape
- Paper and pens
- Chalkboard and chalk or dry erase board and markers

Preparation Needed

None

Class Meeting Outline

Opening Activity (10 minutes)

1. Without introducing the activity, gather students in a circle. Arbitrarily tape or place a colored dot on each student's forehead, so others can see it, but the student cannot.

2. Identify for students which color represents popular students, which color represents outcasts, and which color represents those in between.

   Note: Be mindful of the social hierarchy within your class and assign popular and outcast colors to different students, so that you are not reinforcing actual social standing in the class.

3. **For this game, it's important not to ask other students what color you have.** Instruct students to take 5 minutes to talk or visit with each other, and interact based on the roles each person has.

4. Gather students together in a circle to discuss insights they gained from the activity.

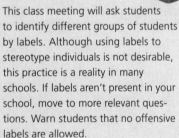

Teacher Tip

This class meeting will ask students to identify different groups of students by labels. Although using labels to stereotype individuals is not desirable, this practice is a reality in many schools. If labels aren't present in your school, move to more relevant questions. Warn students that no offensive labels are allowed.

Discussion Questions (15 minutes)

1. **Could you tell what role you were assigned? What gave you clues?**
2. **How did it feel to do this activity?**

3. **How does being part of a certain social group or having a certain circle of friends affect how you are treated by others? Does it affect how you treat others? How?**

4. **Popularity is an issue that impacts school life everywhere. What makes someone popular? What criteria do people use?** On the board, list traits the class thinks make students popular in your school. Caution students not to mention names or other identifying features of particular students. **In your opinion, which of these traits are positive qualities? Which of these might be considered negative?**

5. **Are standards for popularity the same for boys and for girls? According to research, girls are often selected for popularity on the basis of looks, clothes, and personality. For boys, athletic ability, larger size, and ability to make others laugh often make them popular. In your experience, is that true here at our school?**

6. **Students in many schools have informal labels for different groups of students or cliques. In your opinion, does that happen here? What are some examples? Do you think some of these labels have positive and negative undertones? Why do you think that is? What does that say about traits we value in our culture?**

7. **What is the benefit of being part of a particular social group? Can you be in more than one social group? How do you think these social groups in our school normally get along with each other? What if you don't like the social group you're in? Can you switch?**

8. **How can being a part of a social group sometimes mask who you are as an individual? What do the different social groups have to do with popularity?**

9. **In your opinion, what role does popularity play in bullying situations? Does popularity determine whether someone is more likely to bully others? to be bullied? Does popularity influence what role someone is likely to play in the Bullying Circle? Can bystanders lose popularity if they defend others or tell an adult? Why or why not?**

10. **How can students use popularity as a positive influence in school?**

Wrap-Up

1. **Feeling accepted and respected by others is important to most people. Popularity can be a positive thing if it is used to help others, and not as a means to rule over others who are less popular. Students who are viewed as unpopular may often feel left out. Try to use popularity in a positive way by including others who might not be seen as popular.**

2. Encourage additional questions and comments.

Curriculum Connections

Vocabulary: *clique, criteria, leadership, popularity, social labels*

History/English: Have students research and report on historical figures who "marched to a different drummer" or were "ahead of their time." Oftentimes these individuals were unpopular and were bullied by others because their behavior or their ideas were different from those of most people in their community. Nevertheless, they became successful and made great contributions to our society. Some ideas include Vincent Van Gogh, Albert Einstein, Nelson Mandela, Elizabeth Cady Stanton, Abraham Lincoln, Franklin Roosevelt, Bill Gates, Michael Jordan, Billie Jean King, Harriet Tubman, Amelia Earhart, and Belva Lockwood.

English/Communications: Have students write an answer to this question: What influence do you think the media (print, TV shows, video games, commercials) have on what we view as popular?

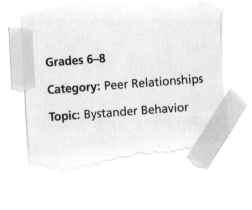

Grades 6–8

Category: Peer Relationships

Topic: Bystander Behavior

Never a Lemming Be!

Background

A bystander is someone who observes an event but does not take part in it. This bystander is typically a chance spectator. The behavior of bystanders is complex and related to several psychological influences on group behavior. Understanding these influences will help students develop into proactive citizens. This class meeting uses examples from the animal world to illustrate concepts about group behavior.

Learner Outcomes

By the end of this session, students will be able to
- define "bystander effect," "herd mentality," and "altruism"
- describe how understanding group behavior relates to bullying prevention

Materials Needed

- Never a Lemming Be! on pages 121–122
- Chalkboard and chalk or dry erase board and markers

Preparation Needed

- Write the three terms on the board: "herd mentality," "bystander effect," and "altruism."

- Make copies of the handout for each student.
- *Optional:* Find pictures of the animals used as examples and post them in the classroom.

Class Meeting Outline

Opening Activity (10 minutes)

1. Assemble students in a circle. **Our class meeting today will focus on several things that influence bystanders' behavior.** Make sure everyone understands the definition of a bystander (a witness or observer). **We will discuss different ways bystanders behave and how bystanders can act as good citizens.**

2. Point out that the terms on the board describe types of group behavior. **Sometimes observing animal behavior can help us understand human behavior.** Explain "herd mentality" and use the following story about the lemming to illustrate this behavior. **The lemming is a small rodent that lives in the Arctic. When the population of lemmings in an area grows too large, lemmings migrate in large groups. If the group of migrating lemmings arrives at the edge of a large body of water, the herd instinct is so strong that the lemmings may press forward and follow their leaders by jumping into the water. Sometimes, this has resulted in their death.** (It is, however, a myth that lemmings "commit suicide" by jumping off cliffs in mass numbers.)

3. **We sometimes use the saying "like lemmings to the sea" to describe group behavior. What does this saying mean?** (The saying is used to describe someone's decision to do something that is not good for him or her just because everyone else is doing it.)

4. Divide the class into small groups. (See pages 13–14 for ideas and strategies for grouping students.) Give each group copies of the handout. Instruct the groups to read the definitions of the terms and then discuss how the term applies to human behavior. **Don't use any names, but discuss with your group examples that you have seen or heard about that illustrate each of these terms. Think of things that happen here at school, at home, or other places you go.**

5. Have students return to the large group for the discussion.

Discussion Questions (25–30 minutes)

1. How does the "herd mentality" sometimes limit what you think you should do to help another student? Even if you *think* you should do something to help another person, how does the herd mentality sometimes *stop* you from taking action?

2. If a whole group of students see that another student needs help and no one does anything, what message does that send to the student in need? to all the students in the group?

3. If no one helps an individual in need, what does that say about the school itself?

4. If you are a bystander when someone is being bullied, how can you overcome the herd mentality and the bystander effect and do something to help the student being bullied? What kinds of things might you do?

5. Why do you think that some people are altruistic and some are not? What do you think makes the difference? How important is altruistic behavior in a civilized society? How about in a school?

Wrap-Up

1. Responding to others who need your help because they are being bullied or having some other kind of trouble can be a really hard thing to do. Being a helpful bystander means thinking for yourself and not just following along with what everyone else is doing. Sometimes it means stepping outside your group and standing with someone else who is all alone.

2. Encourage additional questions and comments.

Curriculum Connections

Vocabulary: *altruism, bystander, bystander effect, citizen, herd mentality, spectator, witness*

English: Have students read the biography of a man or woman who is known for altruism. Alternatively, ask students to research and write a short paper on the source of altruism in human beings.

History: Introduce the following quotation by Albert Einstein: "The world is a dangerous place to live, not because of those that do evil, but because of those who watch and let it happen." Ask students to write a paper about an event in history that illustrates the quotation.

Current Events/Civics: Ask students to watch for news accounts of heroic behavior by adults, children, and/or animals. Have them present an account of the event and discuss why they think it was considered worthy of media coverage.

Social Studies/History: Have each student report on an individual who has contributed in heroic ways to the common good. Examples could include Rosa Parks, Sojourner Truth, Elizabeth Cady Stanton, Susan B. Anthony, Martin Luther King, Cesar Chavez, Booker T. Washington, Jane Adams, and Oskar Schindler.

Never a Lemming Be!

Instructions: Read the definitions of group behavior and answer the questions.

1. Herd mentality. The term "herd mentality" refers to people who go along unquestioningly with popular opinion or behavior even in the presence of potentially dangerous consequences. Taken from the animal world, the term refers to the tendency of herd animals to follow their leaders blindly, even when doing so presents danger. Examples include sheep leaping off a cliff after their leader, wild horses stampeding through fencing or other dangerous obstacles, and lemmings swimming to exhaustion in a group. When have you seen herd mentality in yourself or people you know?

2. Bystander effect. This term refers to a phenomenon whereby a bystander is less likely to help an individual in need of assistance if there are other people present. In fact, the greater the number of people present, the less likely it is that anyone will offer help. Each person assumes that someone else will help so no one does or people see that no one else is helping so they do the same. When have you seen or heard about the bystander effect?

3. Altruism. This term means unselfish concern for others, even when one's own welfare may be compromised. Individuals such as Martin Luther King, Jr., Mohandas Gandhi, and Mother Teresa exemplified altruistic behavior. Altruism is also observable in the animal world. Dolphins, geese, and elephants all exhibit such behavior. For example, migrating geese will leave their flock to stay with a sick or weakened goose. Dolphins cooperate to keep a sick or dying dolphin near the ocean surface so it will not drown. Elephants gather around sick, wounded, or newborn elephants in their herd to protect them from predators. What examples of altruism do you know about? Who is an altruistic person you know about?

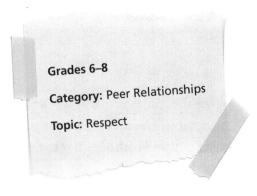

Grades 6–8

Category: Peer Relationships

Topic: Respect

Respect—Who Gets It?

Background

Treating others with respect is an important value, but one that may be difficult for middle school students to practice in the midst of forming social groups and struggling to respect themselves. Every day they observe examples of disrespect by their peers. Cyber technologies (such as cell phones and the Internet) add another layer of complexity because they give students a new, and often anonymous, vehicle for disrespecting others. This class meeting is designed to help students want to treat others respectfully and help them understand how they can do so.

Learner Outcomes

By the end of this session, students will be able to

- describe the importance of treating others with respect
- identify ways they can show respect, both in person and online
- describe the relationship between respect and bullying prevention

Materials Needed

- Paper and pencils
- Chalkboard and chalk or dry erase board and markers

Preparation Needed

None

Class Meeting Outline

Opening Activity (10 minutes)

Teacher Tip

Use the following definition of respect with the group: **Respect:** to have a favorable opinion of a person, to hold a person in high esteem, to admire a person's abilities or personal qualities.

1. Write the word "respect" on the board. **Today we're going to talk about how we can show respect to other people. What does it mean to show respect to someone?**

2. Give each student a sheet of paper. Instruct the students to fold their paper in half and then in half again so that they have four boxes. Tell them to head the boxes: Home, School, Community, Cyberspace.

3. **In each box, list ways that you could show respect to the people you encounter in that place.**

4. Allow students to work individually for a few minutes. Then gather them in a circle to discuss this activity.

Discussion Questions (20 minutes)

1. **What are some ways people show respect?** (Answers might include speaking well of someone, including people, accepting differences, doing nice things for others, being polite, and affirming positive things in other people.)

2. **Do you think you can respect someone you don't like personally? Why or why not? We don't all have to like each other, but we should all be respectful of each other. What are ways you can show respectful behavior toward someone you do not like?**

3. **How do you show respect for your family at home?**

4. **How do you show respect for your friends at school?**

5. **How do you show respect for people you don't know in your community?** (Answers might include basic courtesies like opening doors, not talking loudly on a cell phone in a restaurant or movie theater, not swearing in public, and not wearing revealing clothing to school.)

6. **In what ways have others shown respect to you?**

7. **What are examples of disrespectful behavior that you have observed? In what ways have others shown disrespect to you? How did that feel? What would be examples of disrespectful behavior during a class meeting?**

8. **Some adults believe that young people are no longer being taught to behave respectfully around elders, teachers, and strangers. Do you think this is true? Why or why not?**

9. **What roles do respect and disrespect play in bullying?**

10. **Does the anonymity of the Internet make it easier to be disrespectful? If so, how?** (Because cyberspace allows individuals to hide their real identity, it may encourage people to act disrespectfully without fear of punishment or consequences.)

11. **What kinds of experiences have you had online with people showing disrespect? What does it feel like when someone is disrespectful to you online versus in person?**

12. **How can you make a point of respecting classmates online?** (Ideas might include posting positive messages on individual pages of social networking sites, not forwarding emails or photos without permission, or signing your name when using a concealed email account.)

Teacher Tip

Students may have their own ideas about what it means to be respectful or show disrespect. Ways we are taught to show respect are deeply rooted in our cultural and family traditions. Encourage students to talk about what factors shape their own views and values about what it means to be respectful.

Wrap-Up

1. **Giving and showing respect is an important part of learning to live well with others in this school and in the world. Try using some of our ideas to treat people with respect at home, in school, online, and in the community. We'll discuss our progress in future class meetings.**

2. Encourage additional questions and comments.

Curriculum Connections

Vocabulary: *anonymity, disrespect, respect*

Physical Education/Sports: Discuss the importance of respect for opposing teams as part of good sportsmanship. Practice ways teams show respect for each other. Demonstrate ways people show respect for teammates and in non-team sports. What examples of good sportsmanship have students seen when watching sporting events either in person or on TV? What examples of bad sportsmanship have they seen? If there were consequences, were they fair? What could have been done in those situations instead?

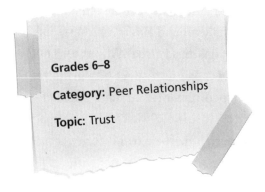

Grades 6–8

Category: Peer Relationships

Topic: Trust

Whom Do You Trust?

Background

Trust is essential to forming healthy relationships. According to Abraham Maslow's Hierarchy of Needs, feeling safe is a basic human need. In order for people to feel safe and live well-adjusted, healthy lives, they need to be able to trust others. The betrayal of trust by a friend is painful, and it may make being able to trust again more difficult. Students can benefit from exploring both how to be trustworthy and how to identify trustworthy adults to whom they can turn when in need. Students who are being bullied should always be encouraged to reach out to a trusted person for help.

Learner Outcomes

By the end of this session, students will be able to
- describe the importance of trust in many aspects of a person's life
- describe the relationship between trust and bullying prevention
- identify two people at school to whom they can turn when a trusted person is needed

Materials Needed

- Blindfolds
- Paper and pencils

Preparation Needed

- Spread out desks/tables and chairs evenly throughout the room, so that there is room for students to walk between them.

Class Meeting Outline

Opening Activity (15 minutes)

1. **Everyone requires trust to live and thrive. What are some examples of things we rely on or trust on a daily basis?** (Answers might include gravity, that other cars on the road will not hit us, that the food for school lunch is not poisoned, that teachers are not aliens.)

2. **A very important aspect of trust is the trust people have in each other. Today, we're going to do an activity that will remind us of our need to trust others.**

3. Split the group up into pairs. (See pages 13–14 for ideas and strategies for grouping students.) Explain to the students that one person in their pair will wear the blindfold. The blindfolded person will place his or her hand on the sighted person's shoulder. The sighted person will then lead the blindfolded person around the room, weaving between the desks/tables and chairs, and back to where they started.

4. Switch places in the pairings to repeat the activity.

5. Gather students in a circle. Distribute paper and pencils and then process this activity.

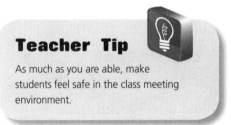

Teacher Tip

As much as you are able, make students feel safe in the class meeting environment.

Discussion Questions (25 minutes)

1. **What was the experience like if you were the guide? What did it feel like to be trusted to lead someone who couldn't see? What things did you do to protect your partner?**

2. **How did it feel if you were blindfolded? What did it feel like to have to trust another person? What things did your partner do that made you trust him or her?**

3. **Let's discuss some of the different aspects of trust. What does trust mean to you?** (Answers may include believing in someone, having confidence or faith in a person, or believing in the reliability and honesty of someone.)

4. **In what people do you have the deepest trust?** Have students list these people on their paper. (Answers might include parents, other family members, teachers, best friends, a religious leader, or a close neighbor.)

5. **What makes some people more trustworthy than others?**

6. **People sometimes betray one another's trust. Why do they do this?** (Answers might include people sometimes make mistakes, friends do it to each other intentionally, people don't understand the effect their behavior might have, or people are inconsiderate of the feelings of others.)

Dig Deeper

Provide a way for students to safely destroy papers they do not want to share so that their inner thoughts are not available to others.

7. **If a friend or someone on your list betrayed your trust, what would you do? If you confided a personal problem to someone on your list and that person did nothing or minimized what you were experiencing, how would you feel? What would you do?**

8. **When the people we care most about betray our trust, it tends to hurt us more. Think about a time when someone betrayed your trust. How did you feel emotionally? physically? Were you able to trust that person again? What did it take to rebuild trust?**

9. **What role does trust play in bullying?** (Possible answers include the bullied student has to trust that someone will do something to stop it; purposefully and publicly betraying someone's trust may be a form of bullying; or you may need to trust your instincts to stay away from people who treat you poorly.)

10. **If you are being bullied, the most important thing you can do is to reach out for help. That takes a measure of trust. You need to be able to trust that the person you tell has the ability to do the right thing when called upon. You also need to trust yourself to know that it isn't your fault that you are being bullied and that you deserve to be safe.**

11. **If you were being bullied, whom would you tell? Which people would you trust to seek out for help?** Have students write five names on their paper of people they could go to. Tell them to be sure to include at least two adults. When students are finished, ask: **Without naming names, what types of people are on your lists?**

Wrap-Up

1. **Trust helps us connect to others in important ways that protect us and remind us we are not alone in the world. Sometimes learning to trust others is challenging, but it is a risk with a big reward. If you need help to stop bullying or with any kind of problem, for yourself or another person, find a trusted person to help you.**

2. Encourage additional questions and comments.

Curriculum Connections

Vocabulary: *betrayal, thrive, trust*

English: Suggest that students write a journal entry about a time when they betrayed someone else's trust or someone betrayed their trust. Have them describe how they felt and how they handled the situation.

Science/Health: Discuss the importance of trust in the development of babies, including how it affects the development of attachment/bonding, empathy, emotional resilience, brain development, and aggression. Explore ways that the absence of trust results in profound challenges in an individual's life. You might use excerpts from research findings to stimulate discussion.

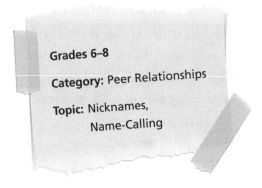

Grades 6–8

Category: Peer Relationships

Topic: Nicknames,
        Name-Calling

Just Kidding!

Background

Nicknames can be a form of endearment, a sign of camaraderie, or an indication that you are liked, belong to a group, or are surrounded by friends who really know you. People use nicknames differently depending on their culture and family traditions—nicknames that might be considered "pet names" or endearing in one culture or family might be construed as negative or even offensive in others. Sometimes, the use of nicknames can be very cruel. Name-calling and the use of negative nicknames can be used to hurt, humiliate, or bully others. Nicknames should only be used in a positive way and when their use is welcomed by the owner.

Learner Outcomes

By the end of this session, students will be able to

- describe the harm that name-calling and inappropriate nicknames cause individuals
- identify positive nicknames
- list ways they can stop someone from using a hurtful nickname

Materials Needed

- Paper and pencils
- Chart paper and a marker

Preparation Needed

None

Class Meeting Outline

Opening Activity (10 minutes)

1. Give each student a piece of paper. **On your paper, make a list of every name or nickname you can ever remember being called. If you've never been called something besides your own name, list names you've heard someone you know being called.** Let students know that they will be keeping this list private and won't be turning it in. Allow students 3 to 4 minutes to create their lists.

2. **Next, make a star next to any nickname that you liked being called. Circle the nicknames that you didn't like or that upset you.** (For students who had no personal nicknames, have them star the names that they felt were positive and circle those they considered negative.)

3. **Make another list of any nicknames you have called others.** Allow another 3 to 4 minutes for students to complete this list.

4. **From this list, draw a star next to any name or nickname that you would like to have been called. Circle the names that you would not want to be called—that you believe hurt another person or were used as put-downs.**

5. Use the lists to motivate discussion of nicknames.

Dig Deeper

Do you use nicknames for students in your class or for other adults in school? In general, the best practice is to refer to students by their given name unless a student specifically asks to be called something else. The use of positive nicknames with students can be viewed as a sign of favoritism and may even be used against a student by peers (teacher's pet). Of course, it is never appropriate for teachers to use negative nicknames for students or to repeat nicknames they have heard other students use.

Discussion Questions (20 minutes)

1. **Look at your first list. Are there more names with stars or circles around them? What about your second list? What makes some nicknames good? bad?**

2. **Some famous people, past and present, are known mainly by their nicknames, part of their names, or even just their initials. For example, Jennifer Lopez is often known as J-Lo, Tiger Woods's full name is Eldrick Tont Woods, baseball player Chipper Jones's real first name is Larry, President**

Theodore Roosevelt was called "Teddy" Roosevelt, and President Franklin Delano Roosevelt was known as FDR.

What are some examples you can think of where famous people or celebrities (past or present) go by nicknames? Encourage students to think of entertainers, sports figures, politicians, or others. Why do these people use nicknames instead of their real names? Why do you think some celebrities change their nicknames or even their names?

3. Have you ever asked people to call you by a name different from your actual or birth name? What are some examples? If so, why did you do that?

4. Sometimes nicknames last a long time, even when they are no longer relevant or seem to fit. For example, there could be someone who was called "Tiny" when he was younger and grew to be 6'4" but still is called Tiny. Why do you think this is? Have you ever tried to change a nickname you were given or gave yourself? What happened? Were you successful? How did that feel?

5. The children's rhyme says, "Sticks and stones may break my bones, but words will never hurt me." In your opinion, is that true? Why or why not?

6. The first thing you might do to stop people from using a nickname that you don't like is simply to ask them to stop. Ask several students to demonstrate an assertive, passive, or aggressive way to ask people to stop using the nickname, and have the group assess responses that each might elicit.

7. Does asking someone to stop usually work? Why or why not? (Responses might include people don't consider others' feelings; asking them to stop might encourage them because they now know that it bothers you; they think it's funny because other people laugh; or it makes them feel important or better than you.)

8. What are some other things you could try to get a nickname dropped? Write students' answers on chart paper and post it as a reminder for the class. (Responses might include ignore the name or don't respond to it; repeat your actual name or one you want to be called; act like it doesn't bother you at all; report the name-calling to an adult at school; or ask another classmate to tell the person to stop.)

9. **Can giving someone a cruel nickname affect how that person feels about him- or herself or affect his or her identity?**

10. **What can you do if you catch yourself referring to someone by a negative nickname? What can you do when it is already said?**

Wrap-Up

1. **Nicknames can be welcomed by the receiver, but often they are not. It is up to the recipient to determine if the nickname is welcome or not. It is never acceptable to give someone a cruel nickname or participate in name-calling. If someone seems distressed by a nickname, don't use it and encourage others not to use it as well.**

2. Encourage additional questions and comments.

Curriculum Connections

Vocabulary: *applicable, cruel, identity, recipient, relevant*

History/English: Have students research and write a report on historical figures who had nicknames. How did they get these nicknames? What impact did the nicknames have on how they were/are viewed by others? In your opinion, is this a positive or negative nickname? In your opinion, does the nickname reinforce certain values or stereotypes? Choose examples of famous as well as infamous individuals to have a variety of positive and negative nicknames. Examples might include Mother Teresa (Agnes Gonxha Bojaxhiu), Dubya (George W. Bush), Babe Zaharias (Mildred Ella Didrikson Zaharias), The Bambino (George Herman Ruth, Jr.), Tokyo Rose (Iva Toguri D'Aquino), Buffalo Bill (William Cody), Calamity Jane (Martha Jane Cannary-Burke), Iron Lady (Margaret Thatcher), Lucky Lindy (Charles Lindbergh), Jackie O (Jacqueline Kennedy Onassis), El Presidente (Fidel Castro), Ike (Dwight D. Eisenhower), The Maid of Orleans (Joan of Arc).

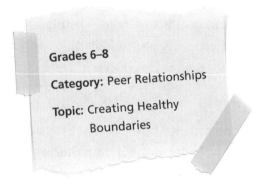

Grades 6–8

Category: Peer Relationships

Topic: Creating Healthy Boundaries

Where Do You Draw the Line?

Background

Bullying prevention involves teaching students to consider how they behave toward others. But it's also important for them to consider which behaviors they will or won't accept from others. Establishing these personal boundaries is a way we protect and take care of ourselves. We need to be able to tell other people when they behave in ways that are not acceptable or when things they do hurt us. Learning how to set boundaries is a necessary step in learning to take care of our own needs. It is our responsibility to decide where we draw the line when others are not respectful and to make choices as to how we treat them. Learning to set clear and healthy boundaries is especially important for students this age as they deal with peer pressure and prepare for dating relationships. This class meeting could be extended to two class meetings.

Learner Outcomes

By the end of this session, students will be able to
- define the term "personal boundaries"
- consider where they draw the line in how they are treated by others
- discuss ways to set limits or draw the line without being unkind or excluding others

Materials Needed

- Chalkboard and chalk or dry erase board and markers
- Setting Healthy Boundaries Worksheet on page 138
- Pencils

Preparation Needed

- Make a copy of the worksheet for each student.

Class Meeting Outline

Opening Activity (15 Minutes)

1. **Many games involve boundaries or rules that set limits on play. For example, sports such as football and tennis have boundary lines that define where participants can play. Can you think of other examples of games where there are either rules or physical boundaries about play?**

2. **What is the purpose of these kinds of boundaries?** (They set expectations so that everyone knows what is acceptable and what is not. Lines define clear limits that show us exactly where we can play.) **What happens when we step on or over boundary lines? How many of you have heard the phrase "crossing the line"? The phrase comes from sports and usually refers to behavior that isn't okay. Can you give some examples of behaviors that might cross the line?**

3. **Today, we're going to discuss ways we create personal boundaries. Personal boundaries are like invisible lines that protect us and help us set healthy limits to deal with behaviors that cross the line for each of us. Setting personal boundaries in our own lives helps us define the way we want others to treat us and when those boundaries have been violated.**

Teacher Tips

Here are more ideas to help explain the concept of personal boundaries:

- Setting and preserving personal boundaries allows you to take care of yourself, resist unhealthy forms of peer pressure, develop strong relationships, and make healthy choices in different social situations.

- Setting boundaries reflects your right to say NO to choices that aren't right for you or that make you feel uncomfortable or unsafe.

- Respecting another's personal boundaries is a sign of respect.

- Boundaries emerge as you learn to value, trust, and listen to yourself. They come from a belief that what you want, need, like, and dislike is important and that you deserve to be treated with respect.

4. **We each need personal boundaries to help us feel safe and keep us healthy. Take 2 minutes with a partner to discuss possible situations where it would be useful or a healthy choice to set personal boundaries about the way people treat you.** Distribute copies of the Setting Healthy Boundaries Worksheet. Give students another 5 minutes to discuss the situations on the worksheet.

5. Bring the students back together in the large group. **Let's hear a few of your ideas about situations when it would be a healthy choice to set personal boundaries for yourselves.** Share group ideas and write them on the board.

Discussion Questions (20 minutes)

1. **How did you determine where you draw the line about the different behaviors that you discussed on the worksheet?**

2. **What behaviors are you not willing to accept from others?** Write the students' ideas on the board.

3. **Close friends share a lot of personal information in confidence with each other.**
   - **What if someone asks you for information about a friend? How do you decide what information should be kept private or confidential?**
   - **What should you do if you made a mistake in sharing too much information about yourself or a friend?**
   - **What if at some time you are no longer friends? What information might another person have about you that could be very embarrassing if that information was made public?**

4. **Where do you draw the line in terms of maintaining a relationship with a person who does not respect your boundaries?**

5. **What are positive things that you can do for yourself when your personal boundaries are not respected in a relationship? How does a person draw the line?** (Responses might include talking about their feelings with a trusted adult or friend, assertively telling the other person how they feel about the situation, considering when to stop being friends with someone, or reporting serious problems to an adult at school or an adult at home.)

6. **Respecting others' physical space or boundaries, even when they are different from our own, shows respect for them. When have your personal boundaries differed from or conflicted with someone else's? What are ways you show respect for someone else's personal boundaries? What is the difference between a personal boundary and excluding or being unkind?**

Wrap-Up

1. **Personal boundaries are individual choices we set for ourselves. They differ from person to person and may change over time. Personal boundaries help us to understand who we are and how we would like to be treated in relationships with others. They help us identify when behaviors cross the line and make us feel uncomfortable.**

2. Encourage additional questions and comments.

Curriculum Connections

Vocabulary: *comfort zone, limits, personal boundaries, physical space, violation/violate*

History/Geography: Have students discuss political boundaries and how countries relate to each other. Is there a formal protocol for establishing relationships with other countries? What courtesy is extended to other countries in establishing relationships? What happens when boundaries are crossed without mutual agreement or there are disputes about what or where boundaries should be?

Setting Healthy Boundaries Worksheet

Instructions: Read each situation. Place a Y, N, or D to indicate how that situation relates to your personal boundaries.

Y = yes, it is within my boundaries
N = no, it is outside of my boundaries
D = it depends

_____ 1. A friend who sits with you at lunch wants to borrow $20. He says he'll pay you back next week.

_____ 2. A girl from your math class asks you to call a boy you know and tell him she wants to go out with him.

_____ 3. Someone whose locker is near yours is always putting his/her arm around you every chance he/she gets.

_____ 4. Your friends are always teasing you about how studious you are.

_____ 5. A girl from English class asks to borrow the paper you wrote so she can get some ideas for hers.

_____ 6. You've been trying to get together with a new friend, and something always seems to get in the way. He's cancelled four times.

_____ 7. Everyone in your group is going to play a practical joke on another group member, and they want you to go along with it. The plan is to fill the person's locker with sand.

_____ 8. A boy you know often walks by you in the cafeteria, smiles, and takes your drink from your lunch tray and doesn't return it.

_____ 9. You befriended someone in a chat room. That person begins to ask you very personal questions.

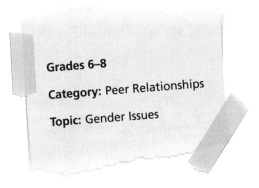

Grades 6–8

Category: Peer Relationships

Topic: Gender Issues

Alike or Different? Can We Be Friends?

Background

Most schools in the United States are co-educational, comprised of both female and male students. How do gender differences impact life at school? How do students this age cope with school in the midst of all the emotional, social, and physical developmental changes during adolescence? Students can benefit from the opportunity to think about these complex issues to better understand the experiences of their own and the opposite gender, and to dispel myths and stereotypes. Creating opportunities for enhanced awareness about similarities between girls and boys can build empathy and promote healthy friendships among all students.

Learner Outcomes

By the end of this session, students will be able to

- identify strengths and characteristics of each gender, from the students' point of view
- discuss similarities between the genders
- describe what "stereotype" means in reference to gender
- discuss boy–girl friendships

Materials Needed

- Chalkboard and chalk or dry erase board and markers
- Paper and pencils
- Coin

Preparation Needed

- Prepare one list of questions for each gender group (see Opening Activity, step 4).

Class Meeting Outline

Opening Activity (15 minutes)

1. **There are ways in which humans are alike, and ways in which we are different. One way we are different is by our gender. How do differences between boys and girls affect your life at school?**

2. Define "gender," "masculine," and "feminine." Gender: whether you are male or female; masculine: having qualities attributed to males; feminine: having qualities attributed to females.

3. Divide the class into two groups, with boys in one group and girls in another. Allow space between the groups so discussions aren't overheard.

4. Hand each group its list of questions.

   a. Have the girls discuss and write down answers to the following:

      - How would you describe girls?
      - What does it mean to behave like a girl or to be feminine?
      - Name the five greatest strengths of females.
      - What would you like boys to know about girls?

   b. Have the boys discuss and write down answers to the following:

      - How would you describe boys?
      - What does it mean to behave like a boy or to be masculine?

- Name the five greatest strengths of males.
- What would you like girls to know about boys?

5. Have the class come together, forming a circle.

Discussion Questions (25 minutes)

1. Make two columns on the board: Boys and Girls. Ask for a volunteer from each group to write the five strengths responses for each group under the appropriate heading.

2. Flip a coin to see whether to begin with the boys or the girls. Start with that group, and then move to the other.
   - **How did your group describe your gender? What does (masculinity/femininity) mean to your group?**
   - **Describe why you chose the strengths you did.**
   - **What would you like the opposite gender to know about you? What are some things you think they may not fully understand?**

Teacher Tips

- You may wish to extend this topic to another class meeting. Don't rush the discussion if it's productive and energizing!

- Be prepared to facilitate discussion that may be lively and somewhat competitive in nature. This class meeting is not designed to divide students or create friction between boys and girls, but to raise awareness and increase understanding. Promote this principle. Remind students to listen carefully to all points of view and to not be judgmental, but open-minded.

3. Ask students to think of things that boys and girls have in common. Have a new student volunteer list them on the board under Similarities. (Responses might include they both like having friends and fun, enjoy sports and hobbies, love their families, get tired and hungry, and want to be liked and appreciated by others.)

4. **Earlier we talked about masculinity and femininity. What happens when boys or girls don't meet the traditional definitions of being masculine or feminine? How are students who seem different than others in their gender group often treated? Describe how this fits into our school's philosophy.**

5. **Whom do girls typically have for friends? What about boys? Think back to kindergarten; are things the same now or have boy–girl friendships changed as you've grown up?**

6. **What is it like for boys and girls to be friends in middle school (easy, difficult, common, uncommon)? Why can boy–girl friendships sometimes be awkward? If you have a friend of the opposite gender, how might others interpret that?**

7. **What can make it easier for boys and girls to be friends?**

Wrap-Up

1. **Gender issues are a part of our everyday life here at school and almost everywhere we go. And as common as this subject is, it is interesting and complex not only during middle school years but also throughout our entire lives. The more we can try to learn about each other, the better we can understand each other in classes, in friendships, in our families, and even in the families that may be in our future. This really helps us to appreciate how we can be so different and so similar at the same time.**

2. Encourage additional questions and comments.

Curriculum Connections

Vocabulary: *feminine, gender, judgmental, masculine, stereotype*

English: Use age-appropriate literature selections to discuss roles of boys and girls, cultural expectations about gender, and the role of gender stereotypes in shaping student behavior and stereotypes.

Social Studies: Have students research human behavior related to certain gender stereotypes that have arisen during this session.

History: Have students explore how gender roles have changed over time. Some examples include voting rights for women and nontraditional careers for men and women (such as males as teachers, nurses, or stay-at-home dads; women as physicians, engineers, astronauts).

Health: Discuss the varying rates of physical and emotional development among youth in this age group.

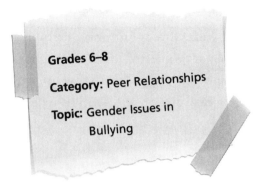

Grades 6–8

Category: Peer Relationships

Topic: Gender Issues in
Bullying

Facts and Myths about Boys, Girls, and Bullying

Background

There are both similarities and differences in boys' and girls' attitudes and behaviors about bullying. This class meeting is designed to help students examine myths and facts about gender and bullying, using data from your own school's Olweus Bullying Questionnaire. In middle school, it is common for students to use gender-related put-downs to bully others. This class meeting will explore this sensitive issue and help students understand the harms that can be caused by their use.

Learner Outcomes

By the end of this session, students will be able to
- describe key facts and myths about bullying and gender
- list key findings from their own school's survey on bullying
- discuss how gender-related put-downs harm everyone

Materials Needed

- Overhead projector, LCD, or printed charts/graphs of school data
- Pencils and paper
- *Optional:* Prizes

Preparation Needed

- Obtain data from your Olweus Bullying Questionnaire.
- Reproduce or summarize selected tables or graphs (see Discussion Questions) on paper or overheads, or show using an LCD projector. (See sidebar for an explanation of SR or HR references.)

Class Meeting Outline

Opening Activity (15 minutes)

1. Tell students that they are going to take a short, ungraded true/false quiz. Ask them to take out a pencil and blank piece of paper. Have them write the numbers 1–8 down the left side of the paper.

2. Read the following "quiz" items or create your own, based on data from your Olweus Bullying Questionnaire. Answers (true or false in parentheses after each statement) are based on national data. If your school data show a different pattern, replace the item with "In our school, _____."

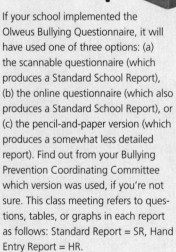

Teacher Tip

If your school implemented the Olweus Bullying Questionnaire, it will have used one of three options: (a) the scannable questionnaire (which produces a Standard School Report), (b) the online questionnaire (which also produces a Standard School Report), or (c) the pencil-and-paper version (which produces a somewhat less detailed report). Find out from your Bullying Prevention Coordinating Committee which version was used, if you're not sure. This class meeting refers to questions, tables, or graphs in each report as follows: Standard Report = SR, Hand Entry Report = HR.

   (1) **Girls hardly ever bully—it's just something that boys do.** (False)
   (2) **Girls bully much more often than boys do.** (False)
   (3) **For boys and girls, the most common type of bullying is verbal bullying.** (True)
   (4) **Relational bullying (using relationships to bully another person) is done by girls but hardly ever by boys.** (False)
   (5) **Boys are more likely than girls to be involved in physical bullying.** (True)
   (6) **Boys only bully other boys. They hardly ever bully girls.** (False)
   (7) **Girls are more likely than boys to tell teachers or a parent if they are being bullied.** (True)
   (8) **Most boys AND girls say that they feel sorry when they see a student being bullied at school.** (True)

3. After reading the eight items, read through the answers quickly without discussing. Have students tally the number that they got right and

wrong. Ask if any students answered all the items correctly. (Consider giving a small "prize" to the students who answered the most questions correctly.)

Discussion Questions (25 minutes)

1. **As you've probably guessed, in today's class meeting we're going to talk about the role gender plays in bullying. I'm sure you all remember taking the Olweus Bullying Questionnaire. Today, we're going to explore some of your answers on this questionnaire, and we're going to look specifically at similarities and differences in girls' and boys' experiences and feelings about bullying.**

2. **Let's review each of these statements and decide which of these are "myths" and which are "facts."**

3. Review statements 1 and 2, which focus on the prevalence of bullying among boys and girls. Both are myths. According to national data, by self-report, boys bully somewhat more than girls, although this does *not* mean that girls do not bully. In some schools, the differences between genders are not great. Review data from your own school's questionnaire about the frequency with which boys and girls bully others (see SR tables 5a and 5b, and graphs 6e and 6f; see HR table E). **When some people think of bullying, they believe it almost always involves boys. Do you agree or disagree? Why do you think that is a common belief? What common attitudes in our culture might affect the incidence of bullying among girls and boys?**

4. Review statements 3–5, which focus on differences in *types* of bullying engaged in by boys and girls. Review relevant data from your own school's questionnaire (see SR table 7 and graph 7; see HR questions 5–12 and 25–32). **What, if anything, surprises you about the types of bullying that boys and girls are involved in at our school?**

5. Select two or three specific forms of bullying where there are differences in rates of bullying among boys and girls. **Why do you think there are differences between boys and girls? What are some examples of relational bullying?** (For example, spreading rumors, or excluding someone from the social group.) **Some people believe that relational bullying, or bullying that**

Dig Deeper

More detailed classroom resources exist for addressing issues of gender-based violence and sexual harassment. Good examples include *Gender Violence/Gender Justice: An Interdisciplinary Teaching Guide for Teachers of English, Literature, Social Studies, Psychology, Health, Peer Counseling, and Family and Consumer Sciences* by Dominic Capello and Nan D. Stein (1999), *Flirting or Hurting?* by Nan D. Stein (1994), and *Safe Dates* by Vangie Foshee and Stacey Langwick (2004).

uses relationships to cause harm, is only something that girls do, but boys do this too.**

6. Discuss statement 6 and note that it is a myth. **Although boys are usually bullied by other boys, girls are bullied by both boys *and* girls.** Review data from your own school's questionnaire (see SR Appendix A: Question/Table 15 and HR question 15). **Why is this? What are some examples of the different types of bullying that boys usually experience from other boys? that girls experience from other girls? that girls experience from boys? that boys experience from girls? Can boys and girls use gender to bully their OWN gender?** (See SR table 8 and graph 8, which illustrate the different types of bullying engaged in by boys against boys, boys against girls, and girls against girls.)

7. Review statement 7 and note that this is a fact. Discuss data from your school's questionnaire (see SR tables 11a and 11b; HR table G). **Why are boys less likely than girls to tell adults if they are bullied? Is there a stereotype that telling an adult isn't "cool" for boys or isn't "macho" or "manly"? Is this healthy? What could be done to help do away with this stereotype at our school?**

8. Review statement 8. Show students relevant findings from your school's questionnaire (see SR table 13, HR table H) and discuss any gender differences in students' feelings of empathy. **How do you explain the differences between the ways boys and girls behave? What are the unspoken rules about the ways that boys and girls are expected to behave when it comes to showing emotions (such as caring or sadness)? Why is it that although most students empathize with someone who is bullied, they often don't do anything about it? How could we make it more likely that students will help stop bullying in our school?**

9. **Often students bully others verbally by making gender put-downs: Students taunt a boy in PE class by saying, "You throw like a girl!" Or a girl sends an IM to her friends saying, "Michelle doesn't have a clue what clothes to wear. She's just like a guy!" What are some other examples? Let's focus on the first example I gave—taunting a boy by saying that he throws "like a girl." Why is this insulting to the boy? Who else might it insult? Is it insulting to girls as well? Why? What could we do to encourage each other not to use these gender-related put-downs?**

Wrap-Up

1. **There are important similarities and differences in the attitudes and behaviors of boys and girls when it comes to bullying. In order to try to reduce bullying in our school, it is important to understand and pay attention to these. It also is important to understand how gender can be used to bully—such as by using gender-related put-downs. Let's encourage each other not to use these, as they harm all of us.**

2. Encourage additional questions and comments.

Curriculum Connections

Vocabulary: *derogatory, empathy, gender, gender differences, myth, relational bullying*

Math: Print out selected tables and graphs from the SR or HR that focus on gender issues (see Discussion Questions) and have students interpret them.

Category

Respecting Differences and Promoting Acceptance

(Three class meetings)

Grades 6–8

Category: Respecting Differences and Promoting Acceptance

Topic: Diversity

Common Ground

Background

We all share basic human needs for food, shelter, acceptance, companionship, and love. The many ways that we express our individuality and diversity as humans (whether in our ideas, interests, preferences, cultural traditions, customs, family structures, or language) can divide or unite us. When these differences are valued and embraced, they add richness and depth to our lives. Additionally, when students understand and appreciate not just diversity, but a sense of their shared existence, it becomes easier to see things from someone else's point of view, to feel empathy for them and to include them—all factors that reduce bullying and increase the chance of individuals defending others. This class meeting is designed to help students realize what they have in common with people who may live entirely different lives across the street or across the world.

Learner Outcomes

By the end of this session, students will be able to
- define diversity
- give examples of commonalities among seemingly diverse people
- describe how possessing an understanding of these commonalities helps students to stand up against bullying

Materials Needed

- Chalkboard and chalk, dry erase board and markers, or easel and markers
- *Optional:* Paper and pencils

Preparation Needed

- Provide enough space and resources for each group of three to four students to work at the board or at an easel. Alternatively, provide paper and pencils for each group.

Class Meeting Outline

Opening Activity (15 minutes)

Teacher Tips

- Be aware of students in your group who have been bullied because they are perceived as being different—whether because of their physical features, abilities, cultural or ethnic background, or social class. Be prepared to address derogatory comments or implications directly: "Those sorts of comments/put-downs/actions aren't accepted here."

- Students with special needs or disabilities are at an increased risk of being targeted by bullying behavior. Be mindful of teaching situations that might set students up for embarrassment or humiliation such as speaking in group activities, reading aloud, responding quickly to ideas, or writing in small groups.

1. **Human beings all have basic needs in common. Food, housing, love, companionship, and acceptance are some examples. Today, we're going to discuss other things we have in common.**

2. Divide students into groups of three or four. (See pages 13–14 for ideas and strategies for grouping students.) Appoint one person per group to record answers on the board or easel (or on the sheet of paper).

3. Instruct each group to create a list of things their group members all have in common. Challenge them to go past obvious things they know or can see, like physical characteristics or extra-curricular activities to more subtle commonalities, such as likes or dislikes, hidden talents, family origin, etc. Give the groups about 5 minutes to complete their lists.

4. Ask each group to repeat this exercise (5 minutes), this time thinking of things group members have in common with other students in their school.

5. Continue the exercise (5 minutes) by asking groups to think of students in a school in a neighboring community. Have students write down characteristics that they have in common with those students. Note: If necessary, to help students with this task, pause before this question to identify a specific neighboring community and provide a bit of background about this community.

6. Gather the groups back together in a circle and have them share their lists.

Discussion Questions (20 minutes)

1. **How many characteristics were the same across groups? How many were different? Were there themes that kept coming up?**

2. Review the definition of diversity with the students.

3. **Even though we are all different, we might have more in common with others than we think.** Challenge students to think of things they might have in common with
   - adults in the school
   - students in a school that is considered a "rival" in sports or academics
   - students their age in another state or country (preferably one they have been learning about or have read about in the news)

4. **The Lakota Sioux Indians have a saying, "Mitakuye oyasin"** (pronounced "Mee-tah-koo-yah o-yah-seen"), **which translates to "all my relatives," meaning we are all related. What does it mean to you that we are all related or interconnected? How might knowing you share the same needs and are connected to a stranger who looks nothing like you affect the way you view that person?**

5. **How might this knowledge help you stand up for someone who is being bullied?**

6. **What responsibility do individuals have to step up and protect those with whom they have apparently little in common? What holds us back from doing this?**

7. **In your opinion, what are some ways our country shows that it appreciates or values diversity? What are ways that our country shows it does not appreciate or devalues diversity?**

Teacher Tips

- Because talking about diversity and differences can elicit strong opinions and reactions, help students differentiate between facts and opinions. Encourage them to state their views as "In my opinion . . ." or "From my experience . . .".

- Invite students to share experiences but provide options for students who don't feel comfortable sharing in front of the group. Give students the option to "pass" during a discussion, write concerns down and give them to you, and discuss feelings with a trusted adult at school.

- If students raise issues that suggest discrimination, discuss these privately with the affected student and follow school policies to protect the student and correct the situation.

Wrap-Up

1. **Though groups of people may appear to be very different from one another, we nonetheless share a common humanity with similar types of emotions, needs, fears, and hopes. I hope you will keep this in mind as you interact with other people who may seem different from you.**
2. Encourage additional questions and comments.

Curriculum Connections

Vocabulary: *diversity*

Social Studies:

- Help students explore the experience of being an immigrant. Invite an adult or high-school-aged immigrant or refugee to speak to your class about his or her experience.

- Participate in Mix It Up at Lunch Day, which helps kids break out of their usual seating patterns in the cafeteria and get to know new people. Information about organizing this activity can be found at www.tolerance.org/teens/.

- Show the film *Let's Get Real.* Students featured in the film discuss racial differences, perceived sexual orientation, disabilities, religious differences, and sexual harassment. Use the film as a starting point for class discussion of these issues. The film can be found at www.newday.com/films/LetsGetReal.html.

- Look for cultural events in your community that will offer an opportunity for your students to sample music, food, or celebrations that are different from their own cultural experiences. Suggest that students make a list of similar and different ways that food, music, and dance are used to mark special events or to celebrate across cultures.

Art: Show examples of art forms from around the world. How are they different and how are they the same? Use this as an opportunity to celebrate diversity among students in the class or school, or as an opportunity to raise students' awareness about how art reflects the diversity of cultures around the world.

Music: Have students listen to music from different countries. What are similarities and differences in the instruments used, the rhythms, the "mood" of the selections?

Grades 6–8

Category: Respecting Differences and Promoting Acceptance

Topic: Diversity

Understanding Stereotypes, Prejudice, and Discrimination

Background

Students are very aware of either belonging or not belonging to groups. For most youth, peer relationships provide positive experiences. But some middle school students experience exclusion, bullying, and teasing. Sometimes this bullying focuses on perceived differences (what they wear, their weight, their race, their cultural heritage, their music, their gender or sexual orientation, their socioeconomic group, or their religion). Bullying motivated by such perceived differences sometimes crosses the line to become discriminatory. What students experience at school, discuss at home, or hear or read in the media builds their understanding about people. This information (or misinformation) impacts their appreciation of those who are different from them.

Learner Outcomes

By the end of this session, students will be able to
- define and give examples of stereotypes, prejudice, and discrimination
- show appreciation and respect for individual differences that occur in their school and in their larger communities

Materials Needed

- Three index cards
- Definitions of stereotype, prejudice, and discrimination (see page 11 for definitions)
- Poster board or chart paper, magazines or clip art files, markers, and basic art supplies for posters

Preparation Needed

- Become familiar with the definitions and concepts in the class meeting. Be prepared to provide examples of each term, including examples from current events.
- Write the three key words and brief definitions on index cards (one word and definition per card). Paraphrase the definitions in language that is developmentally appropriate for your students.

Class Meeting Outline

Opening Activity (25 minutes)

1. **Let's start by reviewing our definition of diversity. What are the benefits of living and going to school in a diverse community?** (Answers might include it increases our opportunities to try new things and ideas, makes our pool of potential friends larger, and helps us see things more clearly from someone else's perspective.)

2. **Our class meeting today will focus on ways that intolerance of diversity separates or divides us from each other and interferes with someone's basic human rights. We're going to talk about how stereotypes and prejudice affect how we get along and can lead to discrimination.**

3. Assign students to three small groups. (See pages 13–14 for ideas and strategies for grouping students.) Give each group an index card. Ask students to discuss the word on their card and come up with two examples. They may have seen these behaviors in their school or community or in the media. Instruct one group member to write their examples on the card.

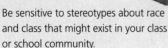

Teacher Tip

Be sensitive to stereotypes about race and class that might exist in your class or school community.

4. Allow the groups time to work. Then have the students assemble in a circle. Call on each group to read its key word and definition and present its examples.

Discussion Questions (15 minutes)

1. **How do people learn stereotypes?** (Answers might include through television or news, from family or members of their community.)
2. **What kinds of stereotypes do you think exist at our school? What are they? How do you know about them? How are they expressed?** Discuss obvious and subtle ways stereotypes can be expressed.
3. **In your opinion, what are some common ways that students your age use differences or stereotypes to bully peers? Why do you think that is?**
4. Divide students into pairs. **Brainstorm ideas with your partner about ways students your age could change one of these common stereotypes.**
5. **Are you aware of any prejudice that exists in our school or community? What are some examples?** Discuss obvious or subtle examples of ways prejudice is expressed.
6. **What are examples of discrimination you think exist in our school or community?**

> **Teacher Tip**
>
> Remind students that derogatory words should not be used and they should describe groups of people respectfully.

Wrap-Up

1. **When we stereotype people, we are not seeing them for who they really are and we are not showing them respect. This can lead to misunderstandings, prejudice, and discrimination. Sometimes bullying can focus on differences or perceived differences as a way of putting others down. We can all work together to stop stereotyping, prejudice, discrimination, and bullying here in our school by working on how we relate to people who are different from ourselves.**
2. As homework, ask students to create a poster or collage that illustrates positive messages to counteract stereotypes, prejudice, and discrimination. At the next class meeting, display the posters and invite students to talk about them as time permits. Alternatively, have students complete this activity in class over a couple of days (as part of art or social studies classes). You may wish to have a schoolwide competition and display the winning posters.

Curriculum Connections

Vocabulary: *covert, cultural heritage, discrimination, diversity, exclusion, human rights, intolerance, overt, perceived differences, prejudice, stereotypes*

Literature: Use age-appropriate literature to stimulate discussion of stereotypes, prejudice, and discrimination. Some examples include *Teammates* by Peter Golenbock, *Number the Stars* by Lois Lowry, and *The Sneetches and Other Stories* by Dr. Seuss.

Social Studies/History:

- Have students explore various religious beliefs, looking for common ideals as well as differences in practices.

- Help students research current events or history for examples of human rights infringement based on discrimination and prejudice. (Examples within the United States: forced relocation of Native Americans, slavery, denial of voting rights to women, Jim Crow laws, treatment of immigrants, racial differences in sentencing criminal offenders. International examples: Darfur, Middle East conflict, Chinese invasion of Tibet, international women's rights issues, ethnic cleansing.) Instruct students to look for strategies used to systematically marginalize groups or to sway public opinion against a particular group of people.

Music: Encourage students to listen to different types of music (from classical to rap). Have them think about these questions: What cultural origins or traditions influenced the music that students like to listen to? How is music used to communicate ideas within a culture? Is it to express feelings or dissent? What roles does music play in celebrations or religious practices in their culture? *I Will Be Your Friend: Songs and Activities for Young Peacemakers,* a free resource from Teaching Tolerance, includes songs on a CD, the lyrics and history of the songs, and class activities that teach more about tolerance.

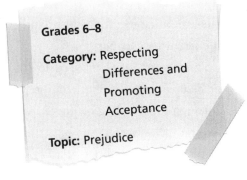

Grades 6–8

Category: Respecting
            Differences and
            Promoting
            Acceptance

Topic: Prejudice

Naming Prejudice

Background

None of us is completely unbiased or free from prejudice. Children begin to formulate biases at an early age. It is important for students to examine biases they hold, understand where they come from, explore what myths are behind those biases, and evaluate them. In addition, students need to learn that they make conscious choices about whether or not to act on these biases in ways that harm or help others This class meeting can be used to address a full range of biases and prejudices common among students in your class (including biases about appearance, gender, real or perceived sexual orientation, social class, religion, cultural heritage, or race). This class meeting will build on the previous class meeting discussion of prejudice.

Learner Outcomes

By the end of this session, students will be able to
- describe the meaning of prejudice
- identify examples of individual and systemic prejudice
- recognize prejudicial behaviors in themselves and others, and work to stop them

Materials Needed

- Current event articles showing examples of prejudice or discrimination
- *Optional:* Stack of current newspapers
- *Optional:* Articles from the 1950s, 1960s, or 1970s that show examples of prejudice or behaviors stemming from prejudice (These articles may be obtained through most public or university libraries with advance notice.)
- Chalkboard and chalk or dry erase board and markers

Preparation Needed

- *Optional:* Allow time to request and obtain old news articles from the library.
- Search for current event articles with examples of different forms of prejudice or behaviors that are rooted in prejudice. Use various sources, including newspapers, periodicals (e.g., *Newsweek, Time*), and the Internet (e.g., nytimes.com, washingtonpost.com, timefor kids.com, teachingtolerance.org). Include examples of overt and covert prejudice as well as individual and systemic prejudice. Provide enough examples for each group of three to four students.
- *Optional:* Prior to this class meeting, ask students to find examples of current event articles that deal with prejudice and bring them to class.

Class Meeting Outline

Opening Activity (10 minutes)

1. Invite students to summarize in their own words the meaning of the word "prejudice." (Answers might include words and phrases such as bias, judging someone before you know them, preconceived ideas, or a negative assumption about a group of people.)
2. **In our last class meeting, we discussed some examples of prejudice. Who can name some examples that we discussed? What are some other examples of prejudice?**
3. **Sometimes prejudice is obvious, or overt, and sometimes it is more hidden, or covert. Individuals can show prejudice but governments and other organizations can show prejudice, too.**

4. Divide the class into groups of three or four students. (See pages 13–14 for ideas and strategies for grouping students.) Give each group one or more current event articles that deal with prejudice or invite students to leaf through newspapers or magazines to find examples on their own. Encourage them to look for examples of both overt and covert prejudice, as well as examples of individual and systemic prejudice.

5. Have each group discuss at least one story and prepare to summarize for the class the examples of prejudice or prejudicial behaviors that they found.

6. *Optional:* Have students look at the examples of prejudice from past decades that you obtained. Compare and contrast the forms of prejudice from the old and new sources.

Teacher Tips

- Be sensitive to the fact that there may be students in your class who have experienced prejudice. Don't force students to share their experiences if they are uncomfortable doing so.

- *Systemic prejudice* is pervasive, established, unequal treatment especially on behalf of governments or institutions.

Discussion Questions (20 minutes)

1. **What causes prejudice?**

2. **What are examples of prejudice among students your age? What are examples of prejudice among students at this school? Are they overt (open, not hidden) or covert (not openly practiced, hidden from view)?**

3. Invite students, if comfortable, to share experiences of prejudice against them. Caution them not to give names or use too many details.

4. **What is your reaction when you hear about prejudice against an individual or a group? How about when you hear about aggression or violence toward another person or group because of the prejudice against them?**

5. **How might you help to stop prejudice? What could you do or say if you hear another student at school expressing or acting on a prejudice?** (Answers might include getting to know people about whom we have prejudicial feelings, checking our own thoughts and feelings, or speaking up against prejudicial remarks from others.)

6. Have students brainstorm responses (such as one-liners) that might be appropriate if they hear others expressing or acting on prejudice. As a class, discuss which are the most appropriate (not rude or derogatory and not likely to escalate a situation), and write them on the board.

7. **How can we work together to stop prejudice in our school? in our community?**

Wrap-Up

1. **We all have the capability to be prejudiced. Ignoring it won't make it go away. Understanding prejudice is an important first step to stopping it. When you hear prejudicial comments and see people being treated wrongly because of prejudice, remember some of the things we talked about today. Try one of those ideas and help out, if you can.**

2. Encourage additional questions and comments.

Curriculum Connections

Vocabulary: *activism, covert, humanitarian, overt, social change, systemic*

History:

- Discuss ways that certain prejudices have diminished or changed over time (marrying across racial or religious lines; adoption by single people; views about homosexuality; women's rights issues; views about the rights of children and youth).

- Have students research and report on examples of systemic prejudice in North America (treatment of native cultures, treatment of women, racial bias and the civil rights movement, sweatshops, child labor).

Category 7

Serving the Community/Reaching Outward

(Two class meetings)

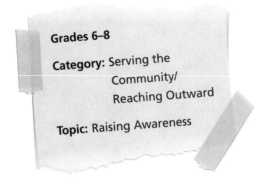

Grades 6–8

Category: Serving the Community/ Reaching Outward

Topic: Raising Awareness

Spreading the Word: Part 1

Background

Rather than receiving a one-time message that bullying is wrong, students will benefit from continuous reminders that bullying behaviors are damaging to individuals, to schools, and to their community. They need encouragement to think of themselves as agents of change who can spread the anti-bullying message throughout their school and to the community beyond. This class meeting will take more than one session, and it may be a cross-curricular activity.

Learner Outcomes

By the end of this session, students will be able to
- identify areas where bullying-prevention awareness is needed in their community
- identify ways they can spread bullying-prevention messages in the community
- plan a project for helping to reduce bullying in their community
- demonstrate cooperative strategies for working together in small groups

Materials Needed

- Copy of the Our School's Anti-Bullying Rules poster (document 8 on the *OBPP* Teacher Guide CD-ROM)

- Chalkboard and chalk or dry erase board and markers
- Computer with Internet access. Preferably, enough computers so students can work in small groups (in the library, classroom, or computer lab)
- Anti-Bullying Campaign Action Plan on page 166

Preparation Needed

- Display the Four Anti-Bullying Rules poster in a prominent place in the classroom.
- Locate public service campaign Web sites such as the National Crime Prevention Council's campaign against cyber bullying (www.ncpc.org/newsroom/current-campaigns/cyberbullying); the National Institute on Drug Abuse (www.nida.nih.gov); Lifelong Literacy (www.loc.gov/literacy); Coalition for Healthy Children (http://healthychildren.ad council.org); The More You Know (TV spots) (www.themoreyou know.com); 15+ Make Time to Listen (family communication) (http://mentalhealth.samhsa.gov/15plus); Teaching Tolerance (www.tolerance.org); Anti-Defamation League (www.adl.org); and, especially, Stop Bullying Now! (www.stopbullyingnow.hrsa.gov).
- Copy the handout, one per group.

Class Meeting Outline

Opening Activity (25 minutes)

1. **In earlier meetings, we have come up with some great ideas and strategies for stopping and preventing bullying here in our school. But as we all know, bullying doesn't just happen here. What are other places in our community where you know bullying happens?** (Locations could include playing fields or community recreation centers, youth groups or centers, school-aged child care, shopping malls, or faith communities.) Write students' responses on the board.

2. **What would be some advantages for you to having anti-bullying messages broadcast outside of school?** (Students might say it would help them feel safe in their community.)

3. **Many of you know about community service campaigns on TV or the radio. These campaigns seek to get important messages out into the community and to work for community change.**

Teacher Tips

- The four anti-bullying rules are defined on pages 51–57 of the Teacher Guide. These rules were initially written for student behavior. Many schools using *OBPP* have extended these rules as expectations for adult behavior as well. How can these rules be extended to the larger school community and your local community?

- Obtain necessary permissions from the school administration and parents for each project.

- Give groups enough time and utilize cross-curricular opportunities. Have groups turn in their action plans for use in Spreading the Word: Part 2.

- Encourage students to view the webisodes from the Stop Bullying Now! Campaign and take part in the discussion questions listed at this Web site.

4. **We'll look at some Web sites to see examples of several different types of campaigns.** Show examples (any except the Stop Bullying Now! site) on a single computer, or divide students into groups and assign each group a site. Ask the following questions:
   - **What are ways these campaigns get their message across?**
   - **What techniques appealed to you? What techniques did you think were most effective?**
   - **What ideas did you get about ways we can get the word out about how harmful bullying is or ways to stop it?**

5. Divide students into groups of three or four. (See pages 13–14 for ideas and strategies for grouping students.) Assign each group a location in your community from the list the class created.

6. Give each small group a space in your classroom with easy access to a board. Ask the groups to brainstorm ideas for a campaign to raise awareness about bullying in their assigned location. Encourage them to write all their ideas on the board (whether they seem practical or not). Allow 5 to 7 minutes for brainstorming.

7. Once groups have generated several ideas, give them another 10 minutes to evaluate and choose one option to develop as a group.

Discussion Questions (10 minutes)

1. **You have just created the beginnings of an anti-bullying campaign. Now let's take a look at the National Bullying Prevention Campaign** (www.stop bullyingnow.hrsa.gov). **This public Web site provides materials that schools can use to create their own bullying prevention campaigns. You can see there are lots of fact sheets, visual aids, PSAs, and other ideas here.** Take time over one or more sessions for students to explore the site's offerings and decide what kinds of information about bullying or materials they could use to develop their campaign ideas.

2. Distribute the handout to groups. Help them develop action plans listing the steps they need to take to implement their plans. Assist students in prioritizing the steps so they experience success. Encourage them to consider community groups that might be interested in collaborating with them on their anti-bullying campaign.

3. Collect the action plans and save them for the next class meeting.

Wrap-Up

1. **Bullying behaviors can be stopped, though it is not always an easy or quick process. Raising awareness in our school and community is an important step toward creating an environment free from bullying.**

2. Encourage additional questions and comments.

Curriculum Connections

Vocabulary: *action plan, campaign, public service announcements, sound bites*

Geography: Have students map the locations in the community where they want to target their campaign efforts. Suggest that they color-code community hot spots for bullying.

English:

- Invite students to write articles on bullying prevention for the school newspaper.
- Have students write stories on the topic of bullying.

Math: Have students develop graphs to depict data about bullying and use these in their campaign projects.

Arts/Drama: Have students create posters or PSAs with an anti-bullying theme.

Social Studies/Community Service: Encourage students to write a letter to community service groups, businesses, media, public officials, or community leaders to enlist their support or collaboration. They might also need to ask permission to use them as a point of access for campaign messages.

Anti-Bullying Campaign Action Plan

Purpose and goal of your campaign (include your location): _____

_____

Directions: Fill in the chart as you discuss and complete each step below.

What steps need to be taken?	Who will take responsibility and complete this step?	What is the timeline for each step?	What resources do you need?	How will you communicate? A. As a group? B. With someone at your chosen location?
Step 1:				A. B.
Step 2:				A. B.
Step 3:				A. B.
Step 4:				A. B.

How will you know your campaign is successful? _____

_____

_____

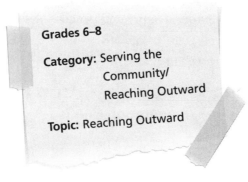

Grades 6–8

Category: Serving the Community/ Reaching Outward

Topic: Reaching Outward

Spreading the Word: Part 2

Background

Students know what national and community educational campaigns are (see Spreading the Word: Part 1), and they have developed action plans for their own anti-bullying campaigns. Now it's important for them to follow through and implement their campaigns in the locations previously identified. Using their action plans, groups will create the resources for their anti-bullying campaigns. This class meeting topic should be spread over several sessions and utilize cross-curricular opportunities.

Learner Outcomes

By the end of this session, students will be able to

- follow the steps they developed to implement an anti-bullying campaign
- create resources for an anti-bullying campaign
- demonstrate further cooperative strategies for working together in groups

Materials Needed

- Each group's action plan from Spreading the Word: Part 1
- Supplies for creating print campaign resources: poster board, newsprint, colored paper, markers, crayons, scissors, pencils

- Supplies for creating audio campaign resources: tape recorders or digital recorders, headphones, paper and pencils for scripts, etc.
- Supplies for creating video campaign resources: video cameras, paper and pencils for scripts, etc.

Preparation Needed

- Set out the campaign resource supplies.

Class Meeting Outline

Opening Activity (30 minutes)

Teacher Tips

- Be sure to provide enough time for this student-centered activity.
- Encourage students to present portions of their campaigns to classmates at regular intervals to get feedback.
- If your school's Bullying Prevention Coordinating Committee has one or more representatives from the community, consider engaging these individuals in this student effort.

1. **Over the next few sessions, you will work in your same group to create anti-bullying campaign resources for your location.** (Resources might include PSAs, posters, articles for local newspapers, bookmarks with slogans or facts to distribute at the local library, a community forum, a Web site or link to the school Web site, posting messages on local billboards, a video project/documentary, buttons, or brochures.)

2. Have the action plans from the small groups available. Recruit a volunteer from each group to briefly summarize the group's plan for the class.

3. Allow students time to further develop each plan and begin creating their resources. Help as needed.

Discussion Questions (10 minutes)

1. Take time each session to discuss group process.
   a. As a way to build camaraderie, encourage group members to begin each session by finding out something new about each other.

b. **What strategies can you use to work together cooperatively and positively in your groups? What are ways to make sure everyone has a role?** Look at ways to encourage nontraditional/nonhierarchical group roles (for example, instead of leader, secretary, and reporter, encourage students to use roles like researchers, questioners, and copy editors).

2. Invite each group to share updates about its campaign to get feedback from peers at key points.

3. Have groups present their completed campaign ideas to the class.

4. Discuss the impact that each campaign might have. **How do you think these resources will help to prevent and stop bullying in your location?**

5. Evaluate how successful each plan is.

Wrap-Up

1. **Your campaigns will help everyone in our community understand more about bullying, its effects, and ways we can all work together to prevent it. What a great way to make our community a more positive and safe place!**

2. Celebrate completion with a special event. Invite parents and community members, and have a special treat.

Curriculum Connections

Vocabulary: *implement*

Social Studies/History:

- Once students have completed their campaign projects, have groups implement the anti-bullying campaign by hanging their posters, scheduling air time to read their announcements on a local radio station, etc. Make sure that parents are aware of these efforts and can help if needed.

- Have students research national and world awareness campaigns throughout history for causes such as AIDS, animal cruelty, homelessness, poverty, and hunger.

Category 8

Using Current Events

(One class meeting)

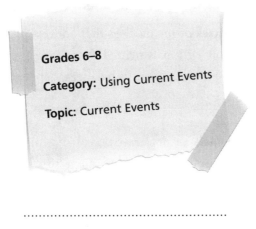

Grades 6–8

Category: Using Current Events

Topic: Current Events

Bullying in the News

Background

The terms "bullying" or "bully" are often prominently featured in media head-lines. It is important, however, to be aware that many of the events described have gone well beyond bullying. In fact, many of these situations (even those that may have begun as bullying) have escalated to become illegal acts of violence, including hazing, assault, child maltreatment by adults, sexual harassment, slander, or murder. Mislabeling aggressive behavior as bullying may not only desensitize adults and students to these more serious acts but also it may minimize the seriousness of these acts. It also may ultimately diminish the seriousness of bullying behaviors (it's "just bullying") and negatively impact bullying-prevention efforts. Current events offer opportunities to reinforce facts and to dispel myths about what bullying is, motivations for bullying, and effective responses.

Learner Outcomes

By the end of this session, students will be able to
- identify types of aggression in current news stories
- use information in a current event to distinguish between bullying, another form of aggression, or illegal behavior
- describe why bullying behaviors are a serious issue not only for youth but also for adults and extended communities

Materials Needed

- Current event articles or media clips that address bullying, other forms of aggression, or topics related to bullying prevention (courage, boundaries/barriers, power imbalances, gender and class issues, relationships, etc.)
- Paper and pencils
- Chalkboard and chalk or dry erase board and markers
- Olweus Bullying Circle diagram (document 18 on the Teacher Guide CD-ROM)

Preparation Needed

- Make sure each group has paper and a pencil.
- Make available current event articles from your school's media center.
- Student homework assignment: Several days before this class meeting, ask students to search newspapers, magazines, and media Web sites that you provided or that they find at home to find current events related to bullying and bullying prevention. Provide students with search parameters, including key search words and a time frame (such as events that appeared within the past week).
- Write small-group discussion questions on the board using the following examples or others as appropriate or relevant:
  - Was this an example of bullying, something else, or both? Describe what the behavior(s) were and why you thought so. Is this behavior illegal? What might be the penalty if it is illegal?
  - Using the Bullying Circle, if relevant, plot out who the "players" were in this story and determine the role they played in this situation.
  - Critique the media presentation of the event or topic. Did it promote a better understanding about bullying behavior, who is involved, or best ways to respond? Why or why not?
  - What, if any, myths or stereotypes did this article contain?
  - What connections can you make between what was described in this article and bullying behavior you see or hear about here at school? in our community?
  - Consider ways that gender and ethnicity came into play in making this story newsworthy. (For example, stories about girls getting into physical fights often are featured

more prominently because that behavior is viewed as out of character; shootings in private schools or affluent suburban areas often get more press because they are seen as outside the norm.)

Class Meeting Outline

Opening Activity (15–20 minutes)

1. **Bullying is a subject that the media sees as newsworthy. This topic gets a lot of press because bullying happens everywhere, and is seen as a huge concern for children and youth.**

2. Have students share or list selected topics or headlines they collected. If you did not have your class do this, set out the examples that you found.

3. Divide the class into pairs or small groups (possibly by event or topic) to summarize and discuss their articles. (See pages 13–14 for ideas and strategies for grouping students.) Ask groups to consider the small-group discussion questions posted on the board. Have groups choose one person to write down their findings.

4. Allow time for group discussion, and then gather the students into a circle to process the activity.

Discussion Questions (25 minutes)

1. **What is one key point your group discovered in your discussion of the news event?**

2. **What is the difference between bullying and a serious act of violence, like a shooting or a beating? What do they have in common?**

3. **In your opinion, did bullying play a role in the event you discussed? If so, how did it factor into that situation?**

4. **In your opinion, what long-term consequences might this event have for those harmed and for the person responsible?**

5. **Bullying behavior in children may become worse and may continue into adulthood. For example, one research study found that boys who bullied**

Teacher Tips

- This topic may need two class meetings. Do the small-group discussion in the first meeting and follow up with reporting by groups at the next class meeting.

- Potential online news sources include the *New York Times* www.nytimes.com; *Newsweek* www.newsweek.com; the *National Post* (Canada) www.nationalpost.com; *Time* www.time.com; CNN www.cnn.com; and *USA Today* www.usatoday.com. Current bullying news articles are also posted on the Olweus Bullying Prevention Program Web site at www.olweus.org.

- In addition to newspapers and news magazines, print resources include women's, parenting, or teen magazines. TV and radio stations also produce online features that may be printed and used.

others in middle school were much more likely than other students to have been arrested as adults. Do any of the articles used in this class meeting show this path in people's behavior?

6. **How do these examples relate to bullying that you have seen around our school?**

Wrap-Up

Dig Deeper

Whenever possible, use current events to highlight bullying-prevention topics for your students. Examples of relevant news topics include acts of courage, whistleblowers, cyber bullying, workplace bullying, school violence, bullying-related suicide ("bullycide"), hazing rituals, local or world events related to civil or human rights, domestic violence, or gang violence.

1. **Bullying is in the news a lot. It's important for us to be good consumers by reading and interpreting those stories, while keeping in mind what we know to be facts or myths about it and the best ways to stop and prevent it. Aggressive behaviors can get worse to become more serious acts of violence, or even violate someone's rights. Understanding the connection between behaviors like bullying and more serious acts of violence can help us all do a better job of identifying aggression or bullying in our school.**

2. Encourage additional questions and comments.

Curriculum Connections

Vocabulary: *abuse, bullycide, consequences, continuum, current events, domestic violence, fact, hazing, human rights violation, media, murder, myth, perspective, protected class, sexual harassment*

English: Link this activity to work on reporting, analysis, and synthesis skills in writing:

- Have students develop a presentation or written report about their small-group findings.

- Encourage students to write about a bullying situation using either a newspaper reporting format or a script for a TV news broadcast.

History/Social Studies:

- Invite students to explore issues such as civil and human rights violations around the world or workplace bullying/harassment laws.

- Have students discuss examples in recent history where aggressive acts by political figures or between nations escalated and led to war or rebellion (such as Idi Amin, Saddam Hussein, war in Iran/Iraq, struggles in the Middle East, rebellions in Burma and Asia).

Science: Ask students to explore and discuss what happens when there is a decreased sense of individual responsibility for the actions a government takes on behalf of its citizens. Some examples include treaties with Native Americans in the United States; concentration camps in Nazi Germany; internment of Japanese Americans in the United States during World War II; war crimes in Vietnam or Southeast Asia; plight of Sudanese "Lost Boys."

....

Notes

....

1. University of Leeds. "Sheep in Human Clothing: Scientists Reveal Our Flock Mentality." *Science Daily* 16 February 2008, 8 September 2008, www.sciencedaily.com/releases/2008/02/080214114517.htm.

2. Pew Internet & American Life Project Parents and Teens Survey, Oct.– Nov. 2006. Based on online teens [n=886]. Margin of error for the overall sample is ±4%. www.pewinternet.org.

3. Ibid.

Recommended Resources

Books

Bloor, Edward. *Tangerine*. New York: Houghton Mifflin, 2006.

Brody, Ed, Jay Goldspinner, and Katie Green. *Spinning Tales, Weaving Hope: Stories, Storytelling and Activities for Peace, Justice and the Environment*. Gabriola, BC: New Society Publishers, 2002.

Capello, Dominic, and Nan D. Stein. *Gender Violence/Gender Justice: An Interdisciplinary Teaching Guide for Teachers of English, Literature, Social Studies, Psychology, Health, Peer Counseling, and Family and Consumer Sciences*. Wellesley, MA: Wellesley Centers for Women, 1999.

Forest, Heather. *Wisdom Tales from Around the World*. Atlanta: August House Publishers, 1996.

Foshee, Vangie, and Stacey Langwick. *Safe Dates*. Center City, MN: Hazelden Foundation, 2004.

Golenbock, Peter. *Teammates*. New York: Houghton Mifflin, 1992.

Lowry, Lois. *Number the Stars*. New York: Random House, 1998.

Spinelli, Jerry. *Stargirl*. New York: Random House, 2002.

Stein, Nan D. *Flirting or Hurting?* Washington, DC: National Education Association, 1994.

Seuss, Dr. *The Sneetches and Other Stories*. New York: Random House, 1961.

Tan, Amy. *The Opposite of Fate*. New York: Penguin, 2004.

Films

Let's Get Real: www.newday.com/films/LetsGetReal.html

Magazines

Newsweek
Time

Music

I Will Be Your Friend: Songs and Activities for Young Peacemakers, a free resource from Teaching Tolerance

Web Sites

15+ Make Time to Listen . . . Take Time to Talk (family communication): http://mentalhealth.samhsa.gov/15plus

Animatics and Storyboards: www.storyboards-east.com/storybrd.htm

Anti-Defamation League: www.adl.org

CNN: www.cnn.com

Coalition for Healthy Children: http://healthychildren.adcouncil.org

Hazelden's *Cyber Bullying* curricula: www.hazelden.org/cyberbullying

Hazelden's *Peaceful School Bus Program:* www.hazelden.org/web/go/peacefulschoolbus

Lifelong Literacy: www.loc.gov/literacy

Mix It Up at Lunch Day: www.tolerance.org/teens

National Crime Prevention Council: www.ncpc.org/newsroom/current-campaigns/bully-prevention

National Institute on Drug Abuse: www.nida.nih.gov

National Post: www.nationalpost.com

New York Times: www.nytimes.com

Olweus Bullying Prevention Program: www.olweus.org

Stop Bullying Now: www.stopbullyingnow.hrsa.gov

The More You Know (TV spots): www.themoreyouknow.com

Time for Kids: www.timeforkids.com

Time magazine online: www.time.com

Title IX: www.titleix.info

United States Department of Education: www.ed.gov/parents/academic/help/adolescence/part9.html

United States Department of Justice: www.usdoj.gov/crt/cor/coord/ixlegal.php

USA Today: www.usatoday.com

Washington Post: www.washingtonpost.com

About the Authors

Vicki Crocker Flerx, Ph.D.

Vicki C. Flerx helped bring the *Olweus Bullying Prevention Program* to the United States and now is a Program Director for the program. She also is a research assistant professor at the Institute on Family and Neighborhood Life at Clemson University. She has expertise in both public and mental health.

Prior to earning her doctorate in public health, Dr. Flerx spent fifteen years as a therapist working in psychiatric settings and focusing on women and youth who were victims of abuse. In addition, she has conducted research in family violence, including intimate partner violence, child abuse, and children exposed to domestic violence. She now trains and consults nationally to support the dissemination of the *Olweus Bullying Prevention Program*.

Dr. Flerx co-authored the *Olweus Bullying Prevention Program* Schoolwide Guide and Teacher Guide, and the *Olweus Bullying Prevention Program Class Meetings and Individual Interventions: A How-To Guide and DVDs*.

Susan P. Limber, Ph.D., MLS

Susan P. Limber is a professor within the Institute on Family and Neighborhood Life at Clemson University. She is a developmental psychologist who received her master's and doctoral degrees in psychology at the University of Nebraska–Lincoln. She also holds a master's of legal studies from Nebraska.

Dr. Limber's research and writing focus on legal and psychological issues related to youth violence (particularly bullying among children), child protection, and children's rights. She directed the first wide-scale implementation and evaluation of the *Olweus Bullying Prevention Program* in the United States and co-authored the *Blueprint for the Bullying Prevention Program* and *Cyber Bullying: Bullying in the Digital Age*, as well as many articles about bullying.

In recent years, Dr. Limber has directed the implementation of the *Olweus Bullying Prevention Program* in the United States. She also provides consultation to the National Bullying Prevention Campaign, supported by the Health Resources and Services Administration. In 1997, she received the Saleem Shah Award for early career excellence in psychology-law policy, awarded by the American Psychology-Law Society of the American Psychological Association (Division 41) and the American Academy of Forensic Psychiatry. In 2004, Dr. Limber received the American Psychological Association's Early Career Award for Psychology in the Public Interest.

Nancy Mullin, M.Ed.

Nancy Mullin is a Program Director for the *Olweus Bullying Prevention Program*. As Executive Director of Bullying Prevention, Inc., she provides consultation and training about bullying prevention in preschool through grade 12. At Wellesley College, she directed the Project on Teasing and Bullying, the Preschool Empathy Project, and coordinated the Massachusetts Bullying Prevention Initiative (the first statewide implementation of the *Olweus Bullying Prevention Program* in the United States).

At Wellesley, she co-authored additional bullying-prevention materials, including *Quit It!: A Teacher's Guide on Teasing and Bullying for Use With Students in Grades K–3*, an approved Olweus supplemental material, and authored the *Selected Bibliography About Teasing and Bullying for Grades K–8* (Revised Edition). Ms. Mullin's nationally known work emphasizes linking bullying prevention themes to classroom curriculum and reducing the negative impact of bullying and gender-role stereotypes on school climate and student performance.

Ms. Mullin co-authored the *Olweus Bullying Prevention Program* Schoolwide Guide and Teacher Guide, and the *Olweus Bullying Prevention Program Class Meetings and Individual Interventions: A How-To Guide and DVDs*.

Jane Riese, L.S.W.

Jane Riese is the Director of Training for the *Olweus Bullying Prevention Program* in the United States as well as an *OBPP* Program Director. She is also a research associate with Clemson University's Institute on Family and Neighborhood Life. Jane became one of the program's first U.S. certified trainers and helped coordinate the first U.S. Olweus Training of Trainers held in 2001 in Pennsylvania. She currently oversees training of the Olweus program for Clemson.

Jane co-authored the *Olweus Bullying Prevention Program Trainer's Manual* and *OBPP* Schoolwide Guide, and contributed to the *OBPP* Teacher Guide. Jane also co-authored the *Olweus Bullying Prevention Class Meetings and Individual Interventions: A How-To Guide and DVDs*.

A social worker and prevention educator since 1982, Ms. Riese created and directed dialogue-based restorative justice programming in her community and was the director of a prosecution-based victim-witness office.

Marlene Snyder, Ph.D.

Marlene Snyder is the Director of Development for the *Olweus Bullying Prevention Program* in the United States as well as an *OBPP* Program Director. She is the national point of contact for Olweus program information, and is a research associate professor at the Institute of Family and Neighborhood Life at Clemson University.

Dr. Snyder consults regularly with a wide variety of professional and community organizations on a range of topics related to bullying prevention and intervention. She is the founding president of the International Bullying Prevention Association. Dr. Snyder has served as a national and international conference speaker, trainer, and technical assistance consultant for educational, mental health, child welfare, and juvenile justice agencies, as well as parent education organizations.

In addition to co-authoring the *Olweus Bullying Prevention Program* Schoolwide Guide and Teacher Guide, and the *Olweus Bullying Prevention Class Meetings and Individual Interventions: A How-To Guide and DVDs*, Dr. Snyder authored a book entitled *ADHD & Driving: A Guide for Parents of Teens with ADHD*.

Dan Olweus, Ph.D.

Dr. Dan Olweus is a research professor of psychology affiliated with the Research Center for Health Promotion (HEMIL) at the University of Bergen in Norway. He has worked on bullying problems among schoolchildren and youth for nearly forty years. His earliest scientific study of bullying was published in Scandinavia in 1973 and in the United States in 1978 as a book titled, *Aggression in the Schools: Bullies and Whipping Boys*.

In the 1980s, Dr. Olweus conducted the first systematic intervention study against bullying in the world, which documented positive effects of what is now the *Olweus Bullying Prevention Program*. The success resulted in Dr. Olweus leading a nationwide government initiative to implement *OBPP* throughout all Norwegian elementary and junior high schools.

Dr. Olweus is generally recognized as a pioneer and founding father of research on bullying problems and as a world-leading expert in this area both by the research community and by society at large. He also was the first to study teachers who bully students.

His book, *Bullying at School: What We Know and What We Can Do* has been translated into fifteen different languages. Dr. Olweus has received a number of awards and recognitions for his research and intervention work, including the "Distinguished Contributions to Public Policy for Children" award by the Society for Research in Child Development (SRCD). He has been a fellow at the Center for Advanced Study in the Behavioral Sciences (CASBS) in Stanford, California.